BACKPACK TO BRIEFCASE

Steps To A Successful Career

Terry Arndt, MBA
John Ricchini, MBA, CPA

Life After Graduation, LLC
5645 Kathryn Street, Alexandria, Virginia 22303
(703) 960-4500 or (877) 569-9816 (Toll-Free)
www.LifeAfterGraduation.com
Info@LifeAfterGraduation.com

USING "BACKPACK TO BRIEFCASE"

"Backpack To Briefcase" is the perfect product to be given as a gift, to raise money for a worthy cause, to increase an organization's membership, or to be used as a promotional device. To learn how you can use "Backpack To Briefcase," or any other Life After Graduation, LLC product, visit www.LifeAfterGraduation.com or contact us toll-free at (877) 569-9816.

OTHER BOOKS BY THE AUTHORS

- Life During College: Valuable Advice & Tips For Success
- Life After Graduation: Financial Advice & Money Saving Tips

COPYRIGHT INFORMATION

BOOK DISCLAIMER

DEDICATION

To Melissa, Tito & Holly: Thank you for all of your love and support. Also thank you for being so patient and understanding. Without you, none of this would have been possible. I love you all very much! - *Terry*

To Jen, Aspen & Sierra: I am sincerely grateful for your patience and encouragement. Thank you for your continued support and for sacrificing your time to help me reach my goals. I love you. - *John*

ABOUT THE AUTHORS

Terry Arndt, MBA

Terry Arndt brings to Life After Graduation, LLC more than 7 years of professional sales and marketing experience; including serving as Assistant Director of Marketing for the National Club Association – an industry trade group representing the private club community, a Technical Sales Representative for EGP, Inc. – a distributor of electrographic products, and a Regional Representative for Consep, Inc. – a manufacturer/distributor of specialty agricultural products. Throughout his professional career, Terry has attended a number of professional training courses in sales, negotiation and business etiquette. His education includes a Master of Business Administration degree from the University of Florida and a Bachelor of Science degree from Washington State University.

John Ricchini, MBA, CPA

John Ricchini brings to Life After Graduation, LLC more than 8 years of accounting and senior financial management experience; including serving as Manager of Financial Planning & Analysis for the University of South Florida Physicians Group, a Senior Healthcare Consultant for PriceWaterhouseCoopers, a Financial Manager for Medaphis Physicians Services Corporation (now Per-Se Technologies) and a Supervising Senior Auditor for KPMG. He is a Certified Public Accountant in the State of Pennsylvania and is currently pursuing a Chartered Financial Consultant designation from The American University. John's education includes a Master of Business Administration degree from the University of Florida and a Bachelor of Science degree in Accounting and Finance from LaSalle University.

TABLE OF CONTENTS

TABLE OF CONTENTS

TABLE OF CONTENTS

TABLE OF CONTENTS

BOSSES

Regardless of all the other skills you may learn from this book, if you do not have a good working relationship with your boss, your chances of being successful in your organization are extremely limited. By reading this chapter you will learn how to develop a working relationship with your boss, how to work with different types of bosses, how to handle conflicts with your boss, as well as how to deal with a difficult boss.

1. WHAT IS A BOSS?

A boss is a person of authority within an organization. This person can be the owner of the company, the president, the chief executive officer, the director of a department, or even the leader of a team. In some cases, particularly in large corporations, an organization may have numerous bosses.

Some common tasks of a boss include:
- Developing goals, strategies, and benchmarks for the organization.
- Delegating responsibilities, authority and resources to ensure that the goals of the organization are accomplished.
- Building relationships with essential customers, suppliers and other organizations.
- Monitoring various legal and legislative issues that influence how the organization is operated, as well as implementing policies to ensure that the organization is in compliance with the law.

- Conducting periodical reviews of the organization including suppliers, customers, and employees.
- Staffing the organization with qualified employees and awarding periodic raises and promotions to minimize turnover, as well as ensuring that employees are satisfied.

2. DEVELOPING A RELATIONSHIP WITH YOUR BOSS

To be successful in your current position and your career, it is essential that you develop a strong working relationship with your boss. Developing a relationship does not mean that you should try to be your boss' friend; rather it means that you should be a good employee. The following bullet points provide tips and suggestions on how to develop a strong working relationship with your boss.

- Understand your boss' role in the organization. What are his responsibilities, who does he answer to, how is his performance judged, etc. By understanding your boss' role in the organization, you will be better able to complete your job in a manner that will best serve his needs, as well as yours.
- Be aware of personality traits and conflicts. For example, what are your boss' pet peeves and whom does your boss not get along with? Knowing this information can help you avoid developing habits or characteristics that may upset your boss.
- Be conscious of your boss' normal schedule. Like you, your boss probably has a regular work routine that he has developed to enable him to accomplish all of his tasks in a set amount of time. For example, if you know that your boss is extremely busy in the late afternoon, avoid disrupting him at this time. Instead, visit with your boss the next morning or consider sending him an e-mail to allow him to address your question/concern at his convenience.
- Be supportive of your boss. Express your satisfaction with your boss and acknowledge his work in front of your colleagues and coworkers.
- Communicate with your boss. Communication is vital to a positive relationship. Therefore, meet with your boss regularly. When sharing information with your boss, be sure to keep your boss posted about important information, such as the status of a project or news about the organization. Also, avoid any delays in passing along information, particularly information about a problem. Learning about a problem is

bad enough, but to learn it from a third party makes you and your boss both look bad.

- Listen to your boss. When your boss is talking or providing instructions, avoid wasting your time and his by asking redundant questions or having to come back to him for clarification. Listen attentively the first time, and ask clarifying questions at that time. However, do not be afraid to ask questions later if needed, as it is best to ensure that you are completing your work correctly.
- Offer to assist your boss. If you believe that your boss is behind schedule or needs help with a project, be sure to offer your assistance.
- Be respectful of your boss' authority. Avoid questioning his decisions or disagreeing with him in front of others. If you have a concern about a decision he has made or you disagree with him, address this with him in private.
- Maintain a positive attitude at work. No one enjoys a negative attitude or constant complaining, particularly a boss.
- Keep the relationship with your boss professional. Avoid discussing personal issues with your boss unless absolutely necessary. Also, limit social activities to work-related functions only.

3. TYPES OF BOSSES & HOW TO DEAL WITH THEM

Management methods vary from boss to boss. Therefore, to develop a strong working relationship with your boss, you not only need to identify the type of management style he practices, but also how best to use that management style to be successful in your career. This section highlights some of the common types of management methods, as well as tips and suggestions that you can utilize to develop a strong working relationship with your boss.

The "Micro-Manager" Boss

The "Micro-Manager" is a person who likes to control every detail of a project to ensure that a project is completed correctly. This type of boss tends to "spoon feed" information to his employees, requires constant feedback on the progress of a project, and questions the methods utilized by his employees to complete a project.

If your boss is a "Micro-Manager," consider utilizing the following tips and suggestions.

- Always reiterate your boss' concerns to express to him that you are aware of his concerns.
- Ask plenty of questions (even if you believe you know the answer) to ensure that your boss understands that you have all the necessary information to complete the project. You may also find it helpful to take notes in front of your boss, as a way to show your boss that you believe the information he is providing is valuable.
- Anticipate questions or concerns that your boss may have about the project you are working on. Have supporting documentation and information available to justify your analysis or the methods that you utilized to complete the project.
- Provide periodic feedback to your boss about your progress on a project.
- When submitting a project, be sure to include all supporting documents and information so your boss is better able to evaluate your work.

The "Hands-Off" Boss
The "Hands-Off" boss is a person that wants his employees to think independently. When he provides his employees a project, he expects little or no interaction with the employee until the project is completed.

If your boss uses the "Hands-Off" management technique, consider utilizing the following tips and suggestions.
- When provided a project, collect as much information from your boss as possible to determine what he expects from the project.
- Use alternative resources, such as your coworkers, for information when you have questions about how to complete a project.
- If you do need to contact your boss for additional information, be sure to limit the number of times you contact him. You may find it beneficial to compile a number of questions to ask at one time.
- When submitting a project, be sure to include all supporting documents and information so your boss is better able to evaluate your work.

The "I Want To Be Your Friend" Boss
The "I Want To Be Your Friend" boss is a person who wants to avoid controversy. When he provides his employees a project, he offers as much or as little guidance as the employee wants. Although he may expect a certain outcome from the project, if the employee does not complete the

project as he intended it to be completed, he would rather complete the project himself versus addressing his concern with the employee.

If your boss uses the "I Want To Be Your Friend" management technique, consider utilizing the following tips and suggestions.
- When provided a project, collect as much information from your boss as possible to determine what he expects from the project.
- Request feedback and advice from your boss as you complete a project to ensure that you are completing it correctly.
- Use subtle techniques when requesting professional criticism. For example, use statements such as "I really value your opinion. Can you tell me where I need to focus my attention, or how to develop the skills I need in order to be a better employee?"
- Because this type of boss is very concerned about your opinion of him, be sure to praise him in front of your colleagues, coworkers and his boss. This will provide him the confirmation that he is accomplishing his goal of being your friend, as well as your boss.

The "Under Qualified" Boss
The "Under Qualified" boss is a person that is concerned that he lacks the qualifications or credentials required to be a boss. In an attempt to correct this, he hires employees that he believes will fill the voids in his qualifications or credentials. Therefore, when he provides his employees a project, he will usually provide very little guidance, as he believes his employees will know what to do.

If you work for an "Under Qualified" boss, consider utilizing the following tips and suggestions.
- Utilize your colleagues, coworkers, or other contacts within the organization, to determine how best to complete a project. In addition, you may find it helpful to request feedback from these people on projects that you have completed to learn how to develop your skills.
- Recognize your boss' accomplishments in front of your colleagues, coworkers, and his boss. Not only will you be building-up his confidence level, but also his trust.
- Take advantage of your boss' concerns about his lack of qualifications or credentials by volunteering to assist him with high profile projects. This will allow you to not only show off your talents and to self-promote

yourself, but also develop the trust of your boss. You may find it helpful to review the "Self Promotion" chapter for more information.

The "Over Achiever" Boss

The "Over Achiever" boss is a person who expects his employees to work as hard, or harder, than he does. He expects the best, and will push his employees to always try harder and to do better. When he provides his employees a project, he will provide the employees all the information they will need to complete the project successfully. In addition, he will provide his employees constant feedback on what they need to do to be successful. However, an "Over Achiever" boss may push his employees too hard to be successful, which can cause tension between him and his employees.

If you work for an "Over Achiever" boss, consider utilizing the following tips and suggestions.

- When provided a project, collect as much information from your boss about what he expects from the project.
- Request feedback and advice from your boss as you complete the project to ensure that you are completing your project correctly.
- Find ways to express to your boss that you are trying to better yourself, such as requesting to attend a training seminar or requesting additional feedback on projects that you have completed.
- Be sure to inform your boss of your extra efforts, such as completing a project over the weekend or working late to finish a project ahead of schedule.

The "Threatened" Boss

The "Threatened" boss is a person that is insecure in his position and is very concerned that he is at risk of losing his job. To maintain control, he will tend to stick to the "status quo" and discourage any new ideas or new ways of thinking. When he provides his employees a project, he outlines exactly what he expects from the project and discourages any diversions from it. The employees that follow his lead will be rewarded, and those that do not are reprimanded or shunned. Working for a "Threatened" boss is a difficult situation to be in for an employee wanting to further his own career.

If you work for a "Threatened" boss, consider utilizing the following tips and suggestions.

- Conduct your projects as your boss has requested.
- Recognize your boss' accomplishments in front of your colleagues, coworkers, and his boss as a method to build his trust. As his trust in you grows, the less of a threat you will become and the more willing he will accept your ideas and suggestions.

4. HANDLING CONFLICTS WITH YOUR BOSS

Occasionally conflicts between you and your boss will occur, such as when your boss declines to approve your vacation request. If handled properly, small conflicts can be resolved without incident. However, if handled improperly, small conflicts can escalate into big problems that can result in you being reprimanded or even fired. Provided below are several tips and suggestions to consider when a conflict between you and your boss occurs.

- Maintain your composure. Becoming angry, frustrated, or emotional will only cause the situation to become worse.
- Determine the cause of the conflict. For example, did you approach the situation in a defensive manner that caused your boss to feel threatened or intimidated?
- Keep the situation in perspective. For example, is a conflict over the use of your vacation time worth creating tension between you and your boss, or worse yet, potentially losing your job?
- Evaluate possible alternatives and resolutions that you can propose to your boss.
- Discuss the situation with your boss. In most cases, taking the time to sit down and talk through the situation will provide a resolution that both you and your boss can agree upon. However, if you are not able to resolve the situation, simply apologize for the situation and move on.

5. DEALING WITH DIFFICULT BOSSES

Dealing with a difficult boss is an uncomfortable situation. Fortunately, there are several things that you can do to resolve this situation. First, follow the advice provided throughout this chapter, such as the tips and suggestions described in the "Developing A Relationship With Your Boss" section or the "Types of Bosses & How To Deal With Them" section. If that information does not resolve the problem, consider visiting with your boss and discussing your concerns. When doing so, approach the subject in a non-threatening manner. If your boss believes you are accusing him of something, his first reaction will be to defend himself. Therefore, offer a non-threatening statement such as: "I have the feeling that I am not meeting your expectations. What can I do differently to ensure I am meeting your expectations?"

If you are unable to resolve the issue with your boss and you are absolutely sure that a change is necessary, consider some of the following options. However, be aware that some of these actions can create additional tension between you and your boss. Therefore, be sure to carefully analyze all possible solutions and potential outcomes before proceeding.

- Ask someone who does not work for your company, such as a family member or friend, for their opinion about the situation.
- Contact a trusted colleague or coworker about the situation and ask for their advice and assistance.
- Discuss the situation with your organization's Human Resources Department. However, be sure to request that any information you discuss be kept confidential.
- If possible, request to transfer to a different department within the organization.
- If all else fails, seriously consider looking for a new position. Life is too short to work in a position that you do not enjoy, adds a significant amount of stress to your life, or limits your career advancement.

BUSINESS MEALS

Business meals are conducted for a variety of reasons, such as entertaining clients, developing professional relationships, or to gather information about a competing organization. Therefore, how you conduct yourself during the meal can often affect the outcome of the meeting. Whether you are the host or the guest, this chapter provides helpful tips and suggestions on how to successfully present yourself in a professional manner during a business meal.

1. TYPES OF BUSINESS MEALS

Business meals can take place during breakfast, lunch or dinner. The time at which a business meal occurs will often determine the length of time, the attendance, the appropriate attire, as well as the expense associated with the meeting. This section provides a number of assumptions that can be made when organizing or participating in a business meal.

Breakfast Meetings

Time: Often begin before the workday starts and can last between 45 to 90 minutes.

Attendance: Well attended because attendees are not required to leave their workplace and a minimal amount of work time is interrupted.

Attire: Business casual to professional.

Expense: Minimal, usually $8 to $15 per person.

Lunch Meetings

Time: Often occur between the hours of 11:30 a.m. and 1:30 p.m. and can typically last between 1½ to 2 hours.

Attendance: Because attendees are required to leave their workplace, attendance can be jeopardized. Often the focus of the meeting will determine the attendance.

Attire: Business casual to professional

Expense: Moderate, usually $15 to $25 per person.

Dinner Meetings

Time: Often occur between the hours of 6:30 p.m. and 8:00 p.m. and can last up to 2½ to 3 hours.

Attendance: Because dinner meetings interrupt an attendee's personal time, dinners tend to only include one to five guests and are often arranged well in advance to accommodate scheduling issues.

Attire: Business casual to professional

Expense: High, usually $35 to $70 per person.

2. PREPARATION

As the host, preparing for a business meal is essential to its overall success. Everything from selecting the location to paying the bill must be prepared for to avoid uncomfortable situations for you or your guests. On the other hand, as the guest, there are a number of items to consider in order to be prepared for a business meal. Whether you are the host or the guest, the following tips and suggestions will assist you in preparing for a successful business meal.

As The Host

- Determine an appropriate date and time to host the business meal. If you are organizing a business meal for several guests, you may find it helpful to contact the primary guests to discuss a date and time that best fits into their schedules.
- Select a restaurant to cater the business meal that you are confident will be able to meet your particular needs. If you are hosting a business meal in a city that you are unfamiliar with, contact guests from the area for their recommendations. In addition, select a restaurant that will be convenient for your guests to attend.

- When hosting a business meal for several guests, consider sending your guests an invitation and request an RSVP at least two days prior to the event to allow sufficient time for organizing the event. In addition, you should consider sending a reminder, or contacting your guests directly a day or two prior to the business meal to confirm attendance.

- Consider a prearranged meal to minimize food preparation time and expense when hosting a business meal for several guests. If you choose to have a prearranged meal, contact your guests about any special dietary needs they may have so that you can plan your menu accordingly. An alternative to a prearranged meal is to offer guests their choice of pre-selected meals, such as a beef, fish or vegetarian dish.

- Contact the restaurant a day or two before the business meal will take place to confirm your reservation and to address any outstanding issues.

- Arrive at the restaurant early enough to arrange for the payment of your bill. If the restaurant will not accept pre-payment, request that the bill be held for payment until your guests have left or instruct your server to present the bill to you when the meal is completed.

- Outline the topics you wish to discuss during the meal to ensure that you achieve your goals for hosting the business meal. You may find it helpful to review the "Introductions & Conversations" chapter for additional information about conducting a conversation during the meal.

As The Guest

- When invited to attend a business meal, contact your host as soon as possible regarding your intentions to attend. Also, if you are not aware of the reason for the meeting, contact your host and request that information in order to be prepared for the meeting.

- Inform your host in advance of any special dietary needs that you have.

- Review information that you know, or that you anticipate, will be discussed during the business meal. You may also find it helpful to review the "Introductions & Conversations" chapter for additional information about conducting a conversation during the meal.

3. GREETING

As the host it is important that you express to your guests your appreciation for their attendance when they arrive. In addition, as the guest, it is important for you to properly greet your host to show your appreciation for being invited to the business meal. This section provides a few tips and suggestions to consider when greeting your guests or host. In addition you may find it helpful to review the "Introductions & Conversations" chapter and the "Non-Verbal Communication" chapter for additional information.

- As the host, it is important that you arrive at the restaurant before your guests arrive and that you wait for them in the lobby. If arrangements have been made to meet at a specific location in the restaurant, such as a private dinning area, wait for your guests at that location.
- If you anticipate being late, contact the restaurant and make arrangements for your guests to be seated and offered drinks and appetizers until you arrive. In addition, be sure to contact your guests and inform them that you will be late and that drinks and appetizers will be available for them as they wait for your arrival.
- As the guest, arrive at the restaurant on time or a little early. If you will be delayed, attempt to inform your host when you plan to arrive. If you are unable to contact the host, call the restaurant and request that they contact your host on your behalf.
- Do not order food until your guests or host have arrived. However, if your guests or host is delayed, ordering a drink is appropriate.
- As your guests arrive, conduct introductions as described within the "Introductions & Conversations" chapter.
- Should your guests or host not arrive, you should wait 15 minutes and then attempt to contact them by telephone to determine when they anticipate arriving. If you are unable to reach them, leave a message informing them that you are awaiting their arrival. Wait at least an additional thirty minutes, at which time it is appropriate to leave a note at the restaurant with instruction that it be given to your guests or host should they arrive after your departure. In the note, inform them the other person(s) that you waited for their arrival, what time you left, and that you hope everything is okay.

4. SEATING

When directed to the dining area, unless assigned seating is offered, determining where to sit can be an uncomfortable situation. This section provides suggestions on how to avoid this situation.

- As the host, it is your responsibility to offer your guests their place at the table. Always offer your guests preferred seating, such as a location with a view or a location that is easily accessible.
- Guests should wait to be seated until the host requests them to be seated or when the host begins to seat himself.
- In most cases, offering female guests their seat first or standing up when a female guest excuses herself is not necessary at a business meal.

5. THE PLACE SETTING

For most business meals, the place setting is fairly standard and self-explanatory. However, the place setting for a more formal business meal may not be so clear and can be intimidating. This section provides several tips on how to properly use the place setting. In addition, a picture of a semi-formal place setting, with a description of the different components, is provided on the next page.

Utensils
- A simple way to remember the layout of a place setting is that all utensils to the right of the plate (besides the knife) are for drinking. All the utensils to the left of the plate are for eating.
- If you are ever unsure of what utensil to use when eating or drinking, wait for your host or other guests to begin and then follow their lead.
- As you begin your meal, use the outermost fork or spoon first and work your way towards the service plate with each course.
- Never place used utensils on the table or tablecloth. Instead, place them on the outer edge of your plate. The knife should rest on the back edge of the plate and the fork and spoon should rest on the sides. When preparing coffee or tea, place the teaspoon on the saucer.
- To inform your server that you have finished your meal, lay your fork and knife next to each other diagonally across your plate (from the 4 o'clock to 11 o'clock position) with the sharp edge of the knife facing away from you.
- Depending on the restaurant, the dessert utensils may or may not be present during the initial part of the meal. In some cases, these utensils are only presented once dessert has been ordered. However, in a formal situation, or when a prearranged meal is being served, guests are aware that dessert will be served by the placement of a dessert fork and spoon located horizontally above the plate. Before dessert is served, the server

will clear any remaining utensils and food from your dining area and move the dessert fork and spoon into their appropriate position.

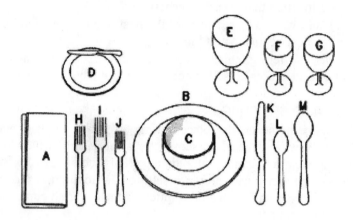

A = Napkin   H = Salad Fork
B = Service Plate   I = Dinner Fork
C = Soup Bowl on a Linear Plate   J = Dessert Fork
D = Bread & Butter Plate with Butter Knife   K = Knife
E = Water Glass   L = Teaspoon
F = Wine Glass (Red)   M = Soup Spoon
G = Wine Glass (White)

Napkin

- After being seated, remove your napkin from the place setting, unfold it, and put it on your lap.
- During the meal, treat your napkin gently. Avoid shaking it out, crumpling it, or stuffing it into your clothing.
- If your napkin falls from your lap, do not pick it up. Instead, request another napkin from your server.
- When excusing yourself from the table during your meal, place your napkin on your chair, not the table.
- After finishing your meal, place your napkin to the left of your plate. Do not refold your napkin; simply lift it from your lap and place it on the table.

6. ORDERING

When attending a business meal, not only is it important to be concerned about what type of foods and drinks you order, but also when it is appropriate to order them. This section provides several helpful tips and suggestions to consider when ordering food and drinks.

Ordering Food

- If you require a special diet, consider contacting your host or the restaurant prior to the business meal and make arrangements to have an appropriate meal available for you.
- When seated at the table, wait to pick up your menu until the host picks up his. Avoid spending too much time looking over the menu. Not only is this rude, but your indecisiveness can be perceived by others as an inability to make decisions quickly.
- Ask the host for recommendations if you are unfamiliar with the restaurant. If your host has a recommendation, seriously consider ordering it as a sign of respect. Also consider asking the server for recommendations.
- As the host, recommend that your guests order appetizers and desserts to prevent your guests from feeling uncomfortable about ordering these items.
- If you have questions about a specific item on the menu, such as how it is prepared or what foods are included, be sure to ask your server to avoid receiving food that you are unable to enjoy. In addition, if you decide that the food you had intended to order is not what you want, have a second item picked out to avoid delaying the ordering process.
- As the host, consider ordering a light meal so you are able to conduct and maintain the conversation, but still participate in the meal. If you are extremely hungry, consider eating a snack prior to your business meal.
- Choose foods that you are familiar with, that are not messy, and that can be eaten easily. For example, avoid foods such as long pastas, seafood in a shell, or that contain melted cheese. In addition, avoid ordering foods that require being handled by your hands to avoid an uncomfortable situation should you need to handle papers after the meal or shake someone's hand.
- As a sign of courtesy to your guests, always allow them to order first.
- Avoid ordering the most expensive item on the menu.

- When you have decided upon your order, close your menu and place it in front of you to signal to your server that you are ready to order your meal.

Ordering Alcohol

The use of alcohol during business meals, particularly dinners, has historically been a part of the business tradition. However, a strong public interest in maintaining a healthy lifestyle, as well as an increased liability risk for businesses that host an event where alcohol is served, has dramatically decreased the use of alcohol during business-sponsored events. When considering ordering alcohol during a business meal, be sure to consider these suggestions.

- Review your company's policies regarding the use of alcohol during business functions, and adhere to them. Your job is not worth losing because of a few drinks. If your company does not have a policy regarding the use of alcohol during business meals, consult your supervisor.
- When asked by your host if you would like a cocktail and you are not sure if anyone else will be ordering one, consider requesting a different drink first, such as a glass of water or soda.
- If you do not drink alcohol, or do not wish to have an alcoholic beverage, do not feel obliged to explain your decision not to drink.
- Should you decide to drink alcohol, be extremely cautious about the amount you drink and know your limits. Even if you assume that you have a high tolerance for alcohol, limit the amount of alcoholic beverages you consume during business-related functions.

7. MEAL ETIQUETTE

Conducting proper etiquette is easy for most people to learn when provided the right tools. However, for some reason, when people are placed in front of food, etiquette is often the last thing on their minds. Conducting proper etiquette while eating is crucial to the success of the business meal, as well as your reputation. This section offers several tips on how to avoid and correctly handle potentially embarrassing and uncomfortable situations that can occur during the dining process.

- Always remember that when the dining table is prepared for dining, that is the activity that should be performed at the table. If an activity or item is not related to the dining process, do not perform that activity or add the item to the table until the dining process is completed.
- As a sign of respect to the host and other guests, turn off your wireless phone or pager before entering the restaurant. If you must have it turned on, set it to the vibrate option. In addition, place items such as a briefcase or files under your chair.
- Avoid resting your elbows or arms on the table while eating. Not only are you interrupting the dining experience of the people next to you, but you also run the risk of causing a spill.
- When asked to pass an item on the table, only reach for the item if it is close to you. If it is not within your reach, request that the person closest to the item pass it.
- Never apply cosmetics or take prescriptions at the table. Excuse yourself and conduct these tasks in the restroom.
- Do not send your food back unless it is inedible. If you must send your food back, discreetly inform your server of the situation in a courteous manner to avoid embarrassing your host.
- When eating, bring your food to your mouth, not your mouth to your food.
- If your food is too hot to eat, allow it to cool. Never blow on your food.
- Never speak with food in your mouth and always eat with your mouth closed. If you are asked a question while you are in the process of eating, finish eating the food in your mouth and then respond. In addition, do not point at your mouth or emphasize your chewing to indicate that you are in the process of eating.
- While speaking during the meal, avoid using your hands to emphasize your conversation while holding your silverware or glassware.
- When bread and butter are included in your meal and a communal butter tray is offered, avoid using your butter knife until you have retrieved butter from the tray. In addition, take a sufficient amount of butter from the tray to accommodate your needs during the meal and then place it on your bread and butter plate. This will avoid the need to continually request additional butter during the meal.
- Do not scrape your plate to get every last morsel of food.
- Never double dip your food.

- Never hold a knife in your hands while eating. When served food that requires cutting, cut enough food for one or two bites at a time, place the knife on the top rim of your plate, and eat the pieces that you have prepared.
- Pace the speed at which you eat to coincide with the speed at which others at your table are eating.
- When eating soup, place your spoon into the soup along the edge of the bowl closest to you. Move the spoon toward the opposite edge until it is about two-thirds full. Lift the spoon from the bowl and rub the bottom of the spoon on the inside edge of the bowl to avoid any drips. Sip the soup from the spoon; do not slurp it. In addition, never lift your soup bowl. To retrieve soup from the bottom of the bowl, tip the bowl away from you slightly.
- Only use your hands to handle food when appropriate, such as sandwiches or berries with stems.
- Never pick up items that fall onto the floor. If food or a piece of your place setting falls onto the floor, request assistance from your server.
- When food falls from your plate onto the table, pick the food up with your silverware and place it on the edge of your plate.
- Should a significant spill occur, such as a beverage or large food item, contain the spill and request assistance from your server.
- When food gets caught between your teeth, do not attempt to remove it at the dining table. Excuse yourself and attempt to remove the item in the restroom.

8. CONVERSATION

The conversation is an important part of a business meal, if not the most important part. Therefore, you are encouraged to review the "Introductions & Conversations" chapter for more information. In addition, provided below are a few tips to keep in mind when conducting a business meal conversation.

- Delay discussing business-related topics until after the meal has been ordered and everyone is able to participate.
- Complete the meal before presenting documents for review or discussion.

- A restaurant is not an ideal location to discuss sensitive subjects. However, if they must be discussed, consider requesting a private dining area to ensure privacy.

9. WHEN THE MEAL IS FINISHED

Once the meal is finished, only a few tasks remain before the meal is complete. This section provides a few helpful tips and suggestions on completing the business meal professionally.

The Host

- As mentioned earlier in this chapter, try to make arrangements prior to the start of the meal for the bill to be paid after your guests have left. If that is not possible, instruct the server to present the bill to you when the meal is completed. If the server accidentally places the bill in front of your guest, immediately correct the mistake to avoid embarrassment.
- Be sure to thank all of your guests for accepting your invitation to join you for the meal and remind them of any follow-up items that you agreed would be completed as a result of your meeting.
- Provide your servers an appropriate gratuity for their service. The standard gratuity is 15% to 20% of the food and beverage bill; however, if your servers provided exceptional service, a larger gratuity is acceptable. In addition, you may find it beneficial to contact the restaurant manager as well, and thank him for the service.

The Guest

- If the server places the bill in front of you by accident, wait for the host to correct the mistake. If the host is not aware that the bill has been placed in front of you or does not make an attempt to accept the bill, avoid opening the bill, but offer to split the expense.
- Before departing, thank the host for the wonderful meal and discussion and reiterate any follow-up items that you agreed to complete as a result of the meeting.
- In many cases the host is responsible for the bill and gratuities associated with the meal. However, you are responsible for services you personally rendered, such as valet or coat service, unless previous arrangements have been made.

BUSINESS TRAVEL

Depending on the type of career you choose, business travel may be a frequent or infrequent necessity. Regardless of the amount of traveling you are required to do, there are important steps and precautions you need to undertake to ensure a safe and problem-free trip. This chapter not only addresses these steps and precautions, but also describes what you can do before, during and after your trip to ensure that your trip is successful.

1. TRAVEL POLICIES & PROCEDURES

Every organization has specific policies and procedures that must be followed when traveling. Therefore, before you travel, it is extremely important that you familiarize yourself with these policies and procedures to avoid confusion and frustration before, during and after your trip. This section provides several helpful tips and suggestions to consider as you review your organization's travel policies and procedures.

- Review your organization's travel policies and procedures thoroughly and be sure to address any questions or concerns that you have with them with your supervisor.
- Develop a clear understanding of how travel expenses are to be paid and reimbursed. For example, will your organization provide you one of their credit cards or are you required to use your own? If you must use your own, be sure that you have sufficient credit available. In addition, if you travel frequently and you are not provided a credit card from your organization, consider acquiring a separate credit card that will only be

used for business-related expenses. This will not only assist you in tracking expenses, but also avoid conflicts with your personal finances. Finally, if for some reason you are unable to acquire a credit card, or you will be incurring a large amount of expenses as a result of upcoming travel arrangements, discuss the situation with your supervisor. In some cases you may be able to receive a cash advance from the organization prior to traveling in order to avoid financial burdens.

- Determine if your organization provides employees a per diem. A per diem is a pre-determined amount an organization will reimburse an employee for expenses incurred during business travel. In some cases, the per diem does not include transportation costs. For example, an organization may provide employees $70 per night for lodging and $45 per day for food. If your expenses for these items exceed the per diem amount, then you are responsible for those additional expenses. Also determine if the per diem is the same for all the cities you will be visiting. Many organizations will adjust the per diem to account for the increased cost of living at various locations.

- Does your organization utilize a travel agency or have an internal department that makes travel arrangements for employees, or are you required to make your own travel arrangements? If you are required to make your own travel arrangements, visit with your supervisor to determine if your organization has preferred status with any airlines, rental car companies, or hotel chains.

- Does your organization provide employees a wireless telephone to use while traveling? If not, and you travel frequently; consider purchasing your own wireless phone for safety. In addition, if you do not travel frequently or you are not able to purchase a wireless phone, consider investing in pre-paid calling cards. They are fairly inexpensive and can easily be tracked for reimbursement.

- Are you able to retain the perks associated with traveling, such as frequent flier miles?

2. PLANNING YOUR BUSINESS TRIP

Planning is essential for a safe and problem-free trip. Therefore, be sure that you provide yourself a sufficient amount of time to prepare for your trip. This section provides several issues to consider that will assist you in preparing for your business trip.

Scheduling Your Travel Time

Despite your best efforts, it is often difficult to predict the amount of travel time required to complete a business-related trip. However, with a little planning, you should be able to develop a good estimate of your travel time. The following items will assist you in scheduling your travel time.

- Determine when you are required to be at your destination. With increased safety policies and procedures being implemented in the travel industry, delays are becoming more common. Therefore, be sure to provide yourself a sufficient amount of time to arrive at your destination. For example, if you are flying to Tampa, Florida for an 8:00 a.m. meeting, you should consider arriving the day before to ensure that you will arrive on time.
- If you are required to travel from one location to another by car or taxi during your trip, consider purchasing a local map or visiting with your contacts in the area to determine the proper amount of travel time. In addition, utilizing on-line mapping services for driving directions is helpful.
- If you have tight flight connections, consider requesting a seat in the front of the airplane to minimize the time it takes to get off the airplane when arriving at your destination.
- If you have important carry-on luggage that you do not want to have checked, consider requesting a seat toward the rear of the airplane. This will allow you to be one of the first passengers on the airplane, which will allow you to secure overhead luggage space more easily.
- Be conservative in your estimates of how long your meetings will last. Although a meeting may be scheduled for one hour, this may not account for additional time requirements, such as delays in starting and ending the meeting.

Making Travel Arrangements

Regardless if your organization utilizes a travel agency, has an in-house department that makes travel arrangements, or you are required to make your own travel arrangements, you have a choice in the travel arrangements that are made. Therefore, consider the following items when deciding upon your travel arrangements.

- Choose a hotel that you are familiar with and that offers the amenities you require when staying away from home, such as a fitness center.

Also, never jeopardize your safety or lifestyle in order to save a few dollars.

- Determine if you will require a rental car or if using a taxi service will be sufficient and more cost effective for your needs.
- Choose an airline and a departure/return airport that is convenient for you to use. For example, just because you can save your organization $100 by flying out of a cheaper alternative airport, your additional travel time and expense to get to and from that airport may outweigh the savings.
- Always bring alternative numbers for hotels, rental car companies, and airline companies should you need to adjust your travel schedule during your trip.

Develop An Itinerary
No matter the length of your trip, always prepare a detailed itinerary for your supervisor, colleagues, family or friends. The more details you can provide, the better. This is not only for your safety, but also allows others to reach you in case of an emergency. Your itinerary should include the following information.

- Meeting times and locations.
- Telephone numbers where you can be reached or where messages can be left for you.
- Details regarding your travel arrangements, such as flight numbers, the rental company you are renting a car from, and hotels where you will be staying.

Work-Related Issues
An essential part of planning for a business trip is ensuring that work-related issues are addressed and resolved before leaving. For example, if your business trip occurs at a time when a project you have been contributing to is being presented, you need to ensure that whoever is presenting the project has all the information they need before you leave. Therefore, as you plan your trip, be sure to keep the following items in mind.

- Organize your office space so that if needed, your supervisor or colleagues can locate needed items easily. As an added perk, returning to an organized office space reduces stress.

- Contact your supervisor, colleagues and coworkers to ensure that they have the required information they may need from you while you are away.
- Resolve as many pending issues as possible to avoid being bombarded with requests upon your return.
- Make a folder of pending items that you can work on while away from the office. Take this folder with you to work on when you have additional time, such as when you experience a delayed flight.

3. PACKING TIPS

Arriving at your destination and realizing that you forgot to pack an essential item is a frustrating experience that can be avoided with a little planning. Therefore, as you prepare to pack for a business trip, be sure to consider the following tips and suggestions.

Personal Items
- Create a checklist of items to bring with you.
- Review your trip itinerary, as well as the weather forecast for your destination to determine what attire you will need to pack. Choose clothing to take with you that is not only versatile and easy to care for, but also appropriate for the weather conditions you will be exposed to. If you need to take heavier items with you, such as a coat or jacket, carry those items with you or wear them while traveling to avoid wasting the limited space in your luggage.
- Limit the amount of luggage you bring, such as one carry-on bag and one small item (i.e. briefcase or purse).
- Always store several plastic bags (grocery or trash) in your suitcase to keep shoes and dirty clothing separated from other items.
- Be sure your luggage is clearly marked inside and outside in case your luggage is lost. Laminated business cards make great luggage tags.
- Prepare a kit of miniature toiletries to save space.
- A small collapsible umbrella and wind-up alarm clock are essential items to take with you when traveling.
- Before packing larger personal items, such as a hair dryer or iron, contact your hotel to determine if these items are available for guests to use.
- Always pack valuables and essential items, such as jewelry and medication, in your carry-on luggage.

Business-Related Items
- Review your trip itinerary to determine what business-related items you need to pack and create a checklist.
- Unless you are able to carry your business-related items with you during your travels, consider shipping these items to your destination prior to traveling to ensure that they arrive at your destination.
- Make a folder of pending items that you can work on while away from the office. Take this folder with you to work on when you have additional time, such as when you experience a delayed flight.

4. TRAVEL SAFETY

Traveling to an unfamiliar area can expose you to some potentially dangerous situations. However, by taking a few precautions, you can minimize your risks significantly and have a safe and enjoyable trip. This section describes several precautions to consider as you travel.

- As mentioned earlier in this chapter, be sure to provide your supervisor, colleagues, family, and friends a copy of your itinerary so someone knows where you are and where you can be reached at all times.
- Familiarize yourself with the areas you will be traveling to. Review local maps and visit with contacts from the area to avoid potentially dangerous areas.
- When choosing a hotel, consider hotels that have an interior entrance to your room versus outside entrances. In addition, request a room on an upper level to minimize the threat of intruders entering your room from a window.
- When entering your hotel room, prop the door open and turn on the lights. Inspect the room for potentially dangerous situations or intruders (i.e. check under the bed, in the closet, and behind the shower curtain). In addition, ensure that all of the windows, as well as the balcony and connecting doors are secured.
- Avoid riding in taxis that appear unsafe or that are driven by someone that makes you feel uncomfortable. Also research the route you will be taking and understand how fares are calculated to avoid being overcharged.
- When renting a car, decline accepting a car that appears unsafe or that you believe you will not be able to maneuver safely. Also, before leaving the rental area, be sure to inspect the car for potentially

dangerous situations or intruders. As an extra precaution, consider choosing the "pre-paid" gas option to avoid the need to stop somewhere unfamiliar to re-fuel your car.

5. RETURNING TO YOUR OFFICE

Returning to your office after a business trip can be an overwhelming experience. Pending projects will need to be attended to, new projects or issues may be awaiting your attention, and you also need to resolve issues related to your trip. Therefore, to minimize feeling overwhelmed, consider implementing the following tips and suggestions.

- Upon returning to the office, develop a list of all the immediate tasks you need to complete, as well as the order in which you need to complete them.
- Address trip-related issues first, such as drafting thank-you notes, submitting an expense report, returning calls, etc. It is best to handle these items first while they are still fresh in your memory.

6. EXPENSE REPORTS

An expense report is a document outlining all of the various expenses incurred by an employee on behalf of the organization for reimbursement. When submitting an expense report, it is important to complete the report as soon as possible to avoid misplacing receipts or other information that account for your expenses, as well as minimizing the time it takes to receive any reimbursements. Therefore, when completing an expense report, be sure to consider the following tips and suggestions.

- Develop a tracking system for your daily expenses, such as listing them on a sheet of paper or handheld personal organizer and placing receipts in your daily planner.
- If possible, consider using a separate credit card for work to assist you in accounting for your business-related expenses, as well as to keep business and personal finances separate.
- Keep a copy of expense reports you submit for reimbursement, as well as supporting documents, in case questions arise or there is a discrepancy in the amount of your reimbursement.

- When submitting receipts that reference your credit card number, cut that portion of your receipt off or cross it out to minimize the threat of unauthorized use of your credit card.
- To ensure you have accounted for all of your expenses during a trip, reconcile your expense report against your credit card statement.
- Never exaggerate or lie on your expense report about the expenses that you incurred during a trip in order to make a few extra dollars. The ramifications of being caught are significantly worse than the gain.
- Staying overnight with a friend or family member instead of at a hotel can save your organization a significant amount of money. Therefore, review your organization's reimbursement policy or contact your supervisor about how situations such as this are reimbursed.

7. COMBINING BUSINESS & PERSONAL TRAVEL

Combining business and personal travel is a great way to save your organization money on airfare and other expenses, as well as minimizing expenses while conducting personal travel. For example, say you are attending a conference in Orlando, Florida. The conference is Wednesday through Friday. The airfare for your trip is $370. However, by extending your stay over the weekend, the airfare is reduced by $180. Therefore, by extending your stay, you save your organization $180 on airfare and you get to enjoy staying in Orlando, Florida over the weekend. However, before you decide to combine business and personal travel, always consult your supervisor to avoid potential conflicts.

COWORKERS

The organization you decide to work for is an important decision that will affect the rest of your life, not only because of the career opportunities that may exist there, but also because of the people you will interact with. In most cases, the group with the most influence on your professional and personal life is your coworkers. This chapter describes how to gain the support of your coworkers, how to develop proper relationships with your coworkers, as well as how to deal with difficult coworkers.

1. GAINING THE SUPPORT OF YOUR COWORKERS

Coworkers have the ability to influence important decisions regarding assignments to team projects, participation in high-level meetings, as well as who is awarded raises and promotions. In order to be successful in your career you need to gain the support of your coworkers. Therefore, this section provides several tips and suggestions to consider in order to gain the support of your coworkers.

- Understand your role in the organization and what is expected of you from your coworkers. You can accomplish this by spending some time with your immediate coworkers and simply asking them what they expect from you.
- Be responsible and dependable. For example, if you are asked to accomplish a specific task, be sure you do it and do it well.
- Become trustworthy. If your coworkers feel that they can trust you, they will be more willing to share valuable information with you.
- Acknowledge your coworker's skills and abilities individually, as well as in front of others.

- Offer to assist coworkers whenever possible.
- Avoid bragging to your coworkers about professional or personal accomplishments. Doing so can create jealousy and may distance you from your coworkers.
- Always do your fair share of work in a group setting and prevent others from carrying too much of the workload.
- Show your coworkers that you value their opinion by requesting their advice.
- Exchange favors whenever possible. Exchanging favors is a great way to develop friendships and build allies.
- Avoid conflicts. If you sense a conflict arising, address the situation immediately and take appropriate actions to resolve the conflict.

2. DEVELOPING PERSONAL RELATIONSHIPS

On average, most employees can expect to work at least 40 hours a week, if not more. This is a significant amount of time to be spending with a small group of people, so it makes sense that developing personal relationships with your coworkers will occur. Although developing personal relationships with coworkers is okay, there are some forms of personal relationships that should be avoided in the workplace. This section discusses favorable and unfavorable relationships for the workplace.

Workplace Friendships

Developing professional friendships in the workplace is perfectly acceptable and is often encouraged by employers to develop a positive work environment for their staff. In fact, some organizations will go so far as to offer their employees activities and functions to help the employees get to know one another, such as social hours and organizational sporting events. Although workplace friendships can be beneficial to the organization, they can also have the opposite effect. For example, if a friend is not performing well at work, that friend may encourage his friends to help him cover-up some of his shortfalls. This type of situation will not only cause tension between friends, but also puts all the parties involved at risk of being reprimanded or even fired. Therefore, when developing friendships with coworkers, it is best to maintain casual professional friendships rather than close personal friendships.

Workplace Cliques

A clique is a small, exclusive group of people who share a common interest, belief or characteristic, such as professional advancement, religion or gender. Many employees become associated with a clique because it gives them a sense of belonging. Although some forms of cliques can offer some benefits to an employee, employers often discourage the development of workplace cliques because they encourage separatism versus a team environment. Therefore, try to avoid becoming an active participant in a workplace clique.

Workplace Romance

Because of the risks associated with romantic relationships in the workplace, such as sexual harassment, most organizations have strict policies discouraging dating between employees. In addition, although difficult to enforce, employers also discourage employees from having romantic relationships with the organization's clients and customers. Even if your organization has not implemented policies regarding dating or other forms of romantic relationships in the workplace, it is best to avoid these situations.

3. DEALING WITH DIFFICULT COWORKERS

Occasionally you will encounter a fellow coworker that you find difficult to deal with, either because of a personality conflict or because of a difference of opinion. Whatever the reason for the tension between you and your coworker, if handled properly, most conflicts can be resolved fairly easily. However, if handled improperly, the situation can escalate into a bigger problem, which can result in you, your coworker, or both of you being reprimanded or even fired. Therefore, when dealing with a difficult coworker, consider the following tips and suggestions.

- Accept the fact that you and your coworkers are different and that you will have differences of opinions.
- Maintain your composure. Becoming angry or frustrated will only cause the situation to become worse.
- Determine the cause of the conflict.
- Keep the situation in perspective. For example, is a conflict over something trivial, such as a coworker drinking one of your cans of soda without your permission worth creating tension between you and a coworker, or worse yet, potentially losing your job?

- Evaluate possible alternatives and resolutions that you can propose to resolve the situation.
- Discuss the situation with your coworker. In most cases, taking the time to sit down and talk through the situation will provide a resolution that you both can agree upon.
- If you have attempted to resolve the situation on your own but have been unsuccessful, consider discussing the situation with your boss or your Human Resource Department.

4. NEW EMPLOYEES

Employee turnover is a normal part of the business world, and part of the employee turnover process is the hiring of new employees. Although most organizations put their new employees through some form of an orientation program to make the transition as easy as possible, new employees will often have a lot of questions as they start their new job. As a fellow coworker, and someone that has recently experienced the feeling of being a new employee, you can offer new employees a wealth of information about the organization that will assist them with their transition. In addition, by offering your assistance, you will be able to start developing a working relationship with these new employees. Therefore, when a new employee is hired, consider implementing the following tips and suggestions.

- Introduce yourself and let the new employees know that you too were recently a new employee of the organization. Often new employees will feel more comfortable asking you questions versus someone who has worked for the organization for several years.
- Stop by and visit the new employees occasionally and see if they have any questions. In some cases, new employees may feel as if they are bothering other employees with their questions and may be hesitant about asking questions.
- Make your new coworkers feel welcomed. For example, invite them to join you and other coworkers to lunch or for a short break away from the office.

ELECTRONIC COMMUNICATION

Over the past decade, organizations have made major advancements in how they communicate and conduct business. The Internet, email and fax machines are just a few of the communication devices utilized by businesses today. The introduction of these tools has not only made communicating more convenient, but also faster. Unfortunately, however, these tools also introduce new security and etiquette concerns for organizations. This chapter will not only provide tips and suggestions on how to use these technologies effectively and appropriately, but also safely.

1. THE INTERNET

The Internet is an invaluable resource of information for organizations. Conducting research for a project, making reservations for travel, or checking on the status of an order are just a few examples of the value that the Internet has provided organizations. However, personal use of the Internet has become a major concern for organizations because of liability and security concerns. The following tips and suggestions can assist you in using the Internet at work.

• Review your organizations' policies regarding the use of the Internet and follow their procedures. Most organizations do not allow personal use of the Internet and may even have tracking systems in place to monitor employee usage of the Internet. If your organization does not allow personal use of the Internet, but circumstances arise that require you to use the Internet for personal use, be sure to request permission before proceeding.

- Even if your organization allows occasional personal use of the Internet, limit your usage to special circumstances only. In addition, never visit web sites that contain controversial materials. The best policy to follow regarding appropriate Internet use is to never visit a web site that you would not want your supervisor to see you viewing.

- Ask your colleagues about common web sites they use to conduct their work. This will help limit the time that you spend searching for appropriate web sites.

2. ELECTRONIC MAIL

Electronic mail, commonly referred to as "e-mail," provides users the ability to communicate with anyone in the world almost instantaneously. Similar to the Internet, e-mail has made conducting business more efficient. However, this efficiency is not without security and etiquette concerns. Because e-mail has become one of the leading methods of communication for businesses, understanding how to effectively use e-mail is extremely important. The following tips will assist you in using e-mail effectively for your work, as well as protecting yourself and your company from the risks associated with its use.

Sending E-mail

When you send an e-mail, the e-mail is not only a reflection of you, but also your organization. Therefore, it is important that every e-mail you send is drafted in a professional manner. This section provides several tips and suggestions that may assist you with this process.

- Be extremely conscious of who you send e-mails to. Mistakes do occur, so before sending an e-mail, always double check the recipient list to ensure the correct recipients are listed.

- Only use the carbon copy (Cc:) or blind carbon copy (Bcc:) options as necessary to inform those recipients that an e-mail has been sent. For example, if your supervisor requests that you send an e-mail, it is appropriate to add him as a (Cc:) or (Bcc:). Also, if you expect responses from multiple recipients, do not add them as a (Cc:) or (Bcc:), but add them as a (To:) recipient. In addition, when using the (Bcc:) option, you may find it helpful to send an e-mail to that recipient prior to him receiving the (Bcc:) e-mail to inform him of why he was added as a (Bcc:).

- Use appropriate words in the subject line of your e-mails. This will help the recipient determine the content of the e-mail easily as well as assist you and the recipient with locating the e-mail at a later time. Also, if you require an immediate response to your e-mail, or a response by a certain date or time, consider placing that in the subject line as well, such as "Annual Report Draft: Respond by June 19th."

- Many e-mail programs offer senders the option to mark an e-mail as "Priority" or "Urgent." Only use these options when absolutely necessary. Frequent use of these options may cause the recipient to begin ignoring these features.

- Keep the content of your e-mail short and to the point. However, if the e-mail is lengthy, consider breaking up the text into smaller paragraphs or using bullet points to make it easier for the recipient to read. This will help the recipient review the information and reply to your e-mail quicker.

- Avoid discussing multiple topics in a single e-mail. If you need the recipient to address multiple topics, consider sending each topic in a separate e-mail. This will help ensure that the recipient addresses each topic completely.

- When writing the content of your e-mail, draft it as you would a business letter.

- If you are sending a purely informative email and no response is needed, state that in the e-mail by writing "For Your Information" or "No Response Needed."

- When sending an attachment, always inform the recipient what the attachment is, what software program will be required to open it and why you are sending it. If the attachment you are sending is a large file and may take some time for the recipient to download, send the recipient an e-mail requesting their permission to send the attachment.

- Always review your e-mail before sending it. Check the content for grammatical errors, look for text that could be misinterpreted by the reader, ensure that the attachment is the correct file, and make sure you are sending the e-mail to the correct recipient. In addition, you may find it helpful to have important e-mails reviewed by one of your colleagues prior to sending it to the intended recipient.

- If you wish to confirm that the recipient receives the e-mail, consider using the confirmation receipt option. Depending on the e-mail program, this will prompt the reader to approve sending you an e-mail confirming that they have received the e-mail. However, use this feature only when necessary as frequent use can become annoying for the recipient.

- Most e-mail programs allow senders to attach an electronic signature to the e-mail. Should you decide to add an electronic signature, only include your contact information. Avoid adding quotes or other information that are irrelevant to the content of the e-mail.

Replying To E-mail

When you receive an e-mail, the person who sent you the e-mail is most likely anticipating a reply from you unless otherwise specified. As described in the previous section, your e-mail is a reflection of you and your organization. How you reply to an e-mail, as well as the speed at which you reply, can influence a person's perception of you. This section provides several tips and suggestions on how to effectively reply to an e-mail. You may also find it helpful to review the tips and suggestions provided in the preceding section, "Sending E-mail."

- Reply to e-mails as soon as possible. A good rule of thumb is to reply to an e-mail within one business day of receiving it. However if an immediate response is not possible, send a short response to the sender informing him that you have received his e-mail and when you intend to send a response.
- If you will be out of the office and are not able to read your e-mails, have your e-mail system set-up to send out an automated "Out of Office" response. Most e-mail systems offer this option. If you are not familiar with how to set up an automated response, contact your Information Technology Department for assistance. Be sure your automated response provides recipients the date you intend to return to your office, as well as an alternate person they can contact should they need immediate assistance.
- When drafting a response to an e-mail, make sure that you have properly addressed all of the sender's questions/issues. You may find it helpful to print the sender's e-mail out and highlight all the questions/issues that need a response. In addition, avoid sending responses that are vague or that may cause additional follow-up e-mails. If you anticipate the sender may have follow-up questions to your response, address those questions in your response.

- Avoid requesting information or asking questions about an unrelated topic in your reply e-mail. Instead, send a separate e-mail addressing the new topic to avoid confusion.
- If you receive an e-mail that was sent to multiple recipients, determine if your reply should be sent to all of the recipients or just the sender. If you are not sure, send an e-mail to the sender and ask which method would be appropriate.

Managing E-mail

Managing your e-mail provides several benefits, such as assisting you in locating important e-mails with ease, as well as freeing up valuable memory on your computer and your organization's server. To learn how to effectively manage your e-mails, contact your Information Technology Department. They will be able to provide you information about developing an e-mail filing system, as well as educate you about the organization's procedures for archiving important e-mails.

Personal Use Of E-mail

Using your organization's e-mail account for personal use should be avoided if at all possible. Even if occasional personal use is authorized, be very cautious. This section provides tips and suggestions to consider regarding personal use of your organization's e-mail account.

- Review your organization's policies regarding the use of the organization's e-mail accounts and follow their procedures. Most organizations do not allow personal use of business e-mail accounts and may even have tracking systems in place to monitor employee usage. If your organization does not allow personal use of the e-mail system, but a circumstance arises that requires personal use of your e-mail account, be sure to request permission before proceeding.
- Even if your organization allows occasional personal use of the e-mail account, limit your usage to special circumstances only. Remember that your organization's e-mail account is the property of the organization and management has the right to view your account at any time. The best policy to follow regarding appropriate e-mail usage is to never send an e-mail you would not be comfortable having someone from your company read.

3. INTERNET & E-MAIL SECURITY

As mentioned throughout this chapter, the Internet and e-mail allow organizations access to numerous resources. Unfortunately, these tools also allow unauthorized access to the organization, such as computer hackers and viruses. Although organizations invest in a variety of tools to protect themselves from these threats, the users are usually the first line of defense. Provided below are tips to assist you in maintaining the security of your organization's Internet and e-mail system.

- Contact your organization's Information Technology Department regarding the organization's security procedures and your role in maintaining them.
- Never download files from the Internet onto your computer as you could introduce a virus or cause the company's server to develop errors. If you need a file from the Internet, always receive authorization first or request that someone from your organization's Information Technology Department download the file for you.
- Do not open suspicious e-mails, particularly if they contain attachment files. Even if you know the person who has sent you the e-mail, do not open the attachment. Contact the person who has sent you the e-mail and ask him what the attachment is. If you ever have a question about the security of an e-mail, contact your Information Technology Department immediately and request their assistance.
- Maintain the secrecy of your Internet and e-mail access passwords.
- If you are away from your office frequently, request that your organization's Information Technology Department establish a recurring password authorization. That way, if someone tries to access the Internet or your e-mail account while you are away from your office, a password will be required before access is granted.

4. FAXES

Fax machines have been used by businesses for many years, and although fax machine technology is older than Internet and e-mail technology, fax machines continue to be a key component to the operation of a business. One advantage of a fax machine, compared to the Internet or e-mail, is that it offers more security; however security concerns still exist. Provided below are tips on how to ensure your faxes are sent correctly, as well as suggestions on how to maintain the security of the information you are faxing.

- Always use a coversheet when you fax a document. The coversheet provides the recipient a quick summary of whom the intended recipient is, the name of the recipient's organization, the department where the recipient works, the fax number, and a description of the information contained in the fax. Your coversheet should also include your contact information.   You may find it helpful to create a fax template to save yourself time when producing fax coversheets.
- The contents of your fax should be easy to read. Avoid using small fonts and sending information that contains a lot of graphics or color. If you are concerned about the readability of a document, photocopy the document, as the reproduction is often a good indicator of what the recipient will receive.
- When sending faxes that are more than 10 pages in length, contact the recipient before faxing the documents to obtain his permission. If the document is not urgent, consider faxing it at a time when the fax machine is not frequently used, such as early in the morning.   In addition, consider mailing the documents or having them sent by courier.
- Avoid faxing confidential information, particularly if you are sending the information to a shared fax machine. If confidential information must be faxed, contact the recipient to inform him when you intend to fax the information.
- When sending important documents, consider programming your fax machine to print a report confirming when the information was sent and received.   Contact your Information Technology Department for assistance in programming this feature. If your fax machine does not offer this feature, contact the recipient by e-mail or telephone to confirm that he has received the information.

HANDLING WORK-RELATED CHALLENGES & SITUATIONS

The ability to handle work-related challenges and situations, such as making mistakes or becoming stressed, is an extremely valuable skill to have. Unfortunately however, the methods for handling these challenges and situations are rarely ever taught in school. If not handled properly, work-related challenges and situations can have a negative impact on your career. Yet, if handled properly, they can be valuable learning experiences. This chapter highlights several important work-related challenges and situations, and the steps you can take to handle them properly.

1. MAKING MISTAKES

No matter how hard you may try, you are going to make mistakes. It is a fact of life. However, if handled properly, mistakes will be nothing more than an opportunity for you to learn how to better yourself. Yet, if handled improperly, mistakes can create serious problems for your career advancement. The following tips and suggestions describe how to properly handle your mistakes.

- Take responsibility for your mistake as soon as you become aware of the mistake; regardless of the size of the mistake. The longer you wait to accept responsibility, the worse the situation may become.
- Apologize when you make a mistake, but avoid making excuses for your mistake. You made the mistake - accept it and move on.

- Learn from your mistakes by clarifying what you did wrong. By doing so, you will be able to avoid making the same mistake again.
- Mistakes do occur, but there is little reason for avoidable careless mistakes, such as misspelled words. Therefore, if you have the tools available to catch mistakes, such as a spellchecker option on your word-processing software, use them.
- Avoid becoming angry or depressed about making a mistake, or dwelling on its occurrence. Instead, consider your mistake a lesson on how you can make yourself better.
- When a mistake has been made, develop suggestions or solutions on how to correct it.

2. EMBARRASSMENT

Experiencing an embarrassing moment is an awkward situation. Regardless of whether the embarrassing situation occurred to you or to someone else, there are things that you can do to minimize the awkwardness associated with this situation. The following tips and suggestions describe a few of these.

- Handle embarrassing situations with confidence and respect. By displaying confidence and respect, you will give others the impression that you are in control of the situation.
- Avoid laughing at another person's embarrassment. However, if that person decides to use humor to divert attention away from his embarrassment, then feel free to make him feel better by laughing with him.
- When an embarrassing situation occurs to another person, divert your attention and the attention of others away from that person to allow that person to regain his composure. Another form of diversion is to divert the attention to you, such as describing an embarrassing moment that you have experienced.
- Apologizing for an embarrassing situation that occurs to you is usually not needed, as this tends to extend the awkwardness of the situation. In fact, the quicker you can regain your composure and divert attention away from the embarrassment, the better.

3. BOREDOM

Boredom is a difficult feeling to overcome particularly when the work you are involved with becomes routine, monotonous or uninteresting. If not addressed, boredom can escalate into much larger problems, such as frequent absences or poor performance at work. Therefore, consider implementing some of the following tips and suggestions should you become bored in your position.

- Diversify your daily schedule to include both the routine and interesting aspects of your work instead of dedicating large amounts of time to one or the other.
- Anticipate when large amounts of boring work will need to be completed and organize your schedule accordingly to allow for frequent breaks or invigorating activities, such as exercise, to help maintain your interest in the work at hand.
- Volunteer for different projects or request new responsibilities to maintain interest in your position.
- Meet with your boss for help in overcoming your boredom. However, avoid using the phrase "bored" when discussing your situation with him. Instead, express interest in "taking on more challenging projects" or "finding ways to diversify your skills."

4. RECEIVING A BAD PROJECT

Unfortunately during your career you will be assigned some projects that you may not necessarily enjoy working on. Although declining to work on the project may be an option, it is usually not the best option. Provided below are a few tips and suggestions to consider when you receive a bad project.

- Avoid complaining to your boss about the assignments he provides to you as complaining is the same as questioning your boss' ability to make good judgments.
- Regardless of the project you have been assigned, always put forth your best effort.
- The best time to approach you boss about future projects is when your current assignment is close to being complete. Use this opportunity to educate your boss on the projects that you would prefer to work on, as well as the projects that you have shown the most success.

5. RECEIVING A VERBAL REPRIMAND

Being verbally reprimanded by a colleague, or one of your clients is far from an enjoyable experience. In fact, it could be considered one of the worst professional experiences you may ever have to endure. Should you have the unfortunate luck of receiving a verbal reprimand, be sure to consider these helpful tips and suggestions.

- A verbal reprimand is never acceptable in a public environment. If you are reprimanded in public, very quickly inform the other person that you wish to conduct the conversation in a private setting. If the individual will not honor your request, then use your judgment to determine if leaving the situation is acceptable.
- Avoid becoming defensive or expressing your anger as this will only cause the other person to become more aggressive.
- Allow the person that is verbally reprimanding you to completely vent his frustrations before speaking or addressing him.
- After the person has finished verbally reprimanding you, paraphrase the main points from the reprimand. Paraphrasing will not only help you understand why the person is frustrated, but also expresses to the other person that you understand what he has told you.
- If you believe that you can resolve the situation easily, then attempt to do so. However, based on the circumstances surrounding the verbal reprimand, you may decide that it is best to resolve the situation at a later time.

6. RECEIVING CRITICISM

Receiving criticism is a common part of any career. Criticism can be positive or negative, but in either case, it is meant to highlight your shortcomings in a manner that will encourage you to improve upon them. The next time you receive criticism, be sure to consider the following tips and suggestions.

- Allow the person that is criticizing you to completely finish before responding, in order to collect all the relevant information.
- Even if the other person is providing you negative criticism, avoid becoming defensive or angry as this may cause the other person to become angry or aggressive toward you.

- Always confirm the information that the other person provided you to ensure that you understand the main points of the discussion.
- Being criticized in public is not acceptable. If you are being criticized in public, very quickly inform the other person that you wish to conduct the conversation in a private setting. If the individual will not honor your request, then use your judgment to determine if leaving this situation is acceptable.

7. HANDLING STRESS

Stress is a mental, physical, and emotional strain that can be caused by any number of situations. Stress is a natural reaction and when controlled, it can be beneficial. For example, the reaction of stress can cause your body to become energized and motivated to correct the situation that is causing the stress to occur, such as completing a difficult project or conducting a presentation to your organization's board. However, stress, when not controlled, can be dangerous as it can cause mental burnout and/or physical exhaustion. Provided below is a list of some of the symptoms of stress, as well as tips on how to control your stress. If you believe you are suffering from excessive stress, consult your supervisor or a healthcare professional for assistance.

Symptoms of Stress
The following conditions may be symptoms of excessive stress.

- **Physical**
  Dramatic weight loss/gain, frequent headaches, constant fatigue, diarrhea, sleeplessness or excessive sleep, muscular tightness or spasms
- **Emotional**
  Easily angered or frustrated, nervousness, irritability, dramatic mood swings
- **Mental**
  Frequently confused, lack of interest in previously entertaining activities, loss of concentration, forgetfulness

Coping With Stress
Although the most desirable situation would be to rid yourself of the situation that is causing you stress, this may not always be an option. If you are not able to rid yourself of the situation that is causing you stress, then

consider utilizing some of the following tips as methods to cope with your stress.

- Get organized and avoid procrastinating. Not being able to manage your time effectively is a major cause of stress.
- Keep negative situations in perspective.
- Avoid dwelling on large tasks that need to be completed. Instead, develop a plan to complete smaller tasks that will eventually allow you to complete larger tasks.
- Maintain a healthy lifestyle. The better you feel physically, the better you will feel mentally. In addition, exercising is a great release of tension and stress. See the following section, "Becoming Physically Active" for further information.
- Avoid working on difficult problems for long periods of time. Take frequent breaks and do something you enjoy.
- Schedule fun, relaxing activities into your weekly schedule.

8. BECOMING PHYSICALLY ACTIVE

Being active and maintaining a regular exercise program is important for overall physical and mental strength. During college, adding physical activity, such as walking between classes, was probably not that difficult. Unfortunately, when people make the transition from college to work, they often do not realize how much their physical activity has been reduced until it is too late. This section provides a few tips and suggestions on how to add more physical activity into your daily schedule. Please remember that the following information is only provided as a guide and is not a substitute for professional medical advice or treatment. If you are concerned about starting an exercise program, you should consult a professional trainer or healthcare professional.

- Without some type of program to follow, you can loose focus on what you are trying to accomplish and may find it difficult to exercise regularly. Therefore, develop an exercise program that you can follow and be sure to develop goals for you to accomplish. There are a number of great resources on developing exercise programs available on-line or in your local library or bookstore. In addition, a healthcare professional or professional trainer can assist you in developing an exercise program that is best for you.

- Contact your organization's Human Resource Department about possible discounted membership programs offered to employees at local athletic facilities.
- Create a progress report of your exercise program and place it in a location that you will see frequently. Progress reports are great motivators and can also provide positive reinforcement. You can chart your progress by using a notebook, a poster board, a calendar, or even your computer.
- If possible consider walking or biking to work versus taking the bus or driving.
- Find a partner to exercise with. Having someone else dependent on you for working out is a great motivator. Therefore, invite a colleague, coworker or friend that shares your interest in maintaining a healthy lifestyle to exercise with you.
- Get involved with group activities, such as a community football or softball league. If your organization does not already have a team, consider coordinating one.

INTRODUCTIONS
& CONVERSATIONS

One of the most uncomfortable situations people experience is being placed in an environment with other people they are not familiar with, such as an industry seminar or luncheon. A common reaction to this situation is to stand or sit quietly by yourself and to wait for someone to start a conversation with you. However, by initiating, developing and maintaining a conversation, you not only develop your networking skills, but you also develop a reputation as someone who is confident and secure. This section will provide tips and suggestions on how to properly initiate, develop and maintain your conversation skills.

1. DEVELOP A GOAL

Before initiating a conversation, determine what you want to accomplish from the conversation. Are you trying to locate potential clients? Are you gathering information about a competitor's new product? Or are you simply interested in participating in casual conversation? Whatever the reason for initiating a conversation, make sure your goal is clear. By doing so, you will be better able to control the conversation, as well as fulfill your needs.

2. INTRODUCTION

An introduction is the first step in the process of developing a conversation. Because the introduction sets the stage for the remainder of the conversation, it is important that the introduction be conducted properly.

Introducing Yourself
When you are in a situation where no one is available to introduce you, or if someone is available to introduce you but has forgotten to do so, it is your responsibility to introduce yourself. The following information contains tips on how you should introduce yourself in a standing or sitting situation.

When Standing
When you are in an environment where conversations will take place while standing up, such as at a business conference or reception, you may find these tips helpful in initiating a conversation.
- Look around the room and make eye contact with someone.
- Smile, walk over to them and offer your hand for a handshake. You may find it helpful to review the "Non-Verbal Communication" chapter for tips on effective handshakes.
- Begin the conversation with a short introduction, such as "Hello, my name is _____. How are you doing?"
- Address the other person by the name the he provides you. For example, if during the introduction the other person states his name as Mr. Robert Smith, refer to him as Mr. Smith until he instructs you to do otherwise. However, if he offers his name as Robert Smith, then it is appropriate for you to refer to him as Robert.

When Sitting
When you are in an environment where conversations will take place while sitting down, such as at a luncheon, you may find these tips helpful in initiating a conversation.
- Avoid initiating a conversation with a person some distance from you, such as across the table. Maintaining a conversation at a distance can be difficult when others around you are also engaging in conversations. Instead, focus on developing a conversation with individuals next to you. However, if there are a limited number of people in your vicinity and the environment allows for a group conversation, you may find it helpful to review the "Group Conversations" section located later in this chapter.
- When you are ready to initiate a conversation, make eye contact with the other person.
- If appropriate, smile and offer your hand for a handshake. For example, if during a luncheon the meal has already been served and eating has proceeded, shaking hands is not appropriate. You may find it helpful to

review the "Non-Verbal Communication" chapter for tips on effective handshakes.
- Begin the conversation with a short introduction, such as "Hello, my name is _____. How are you doing?"
- Address the other person by the name he provides you, as described in the "*When Sitting*" section located on the previous page.

When You Are Being Introduced

When another person is introducing you, you are allowing that person to be your representative. However, it is still your responsibility to make sure that this individual represents you correctly. The following tips will ensure that you are introduced correctly.

- Take a moment to visit with the person that will be introducing you and educate him about yourself, such as the pronunciation of your name, how you prefer to be addressed, what your title is, who you work for, and why you are at this particular event.
- If time permits, you may also want to provide him a few interesting facts about yourself, such as where you are from, what projects you have worked on, and what activities you like to participate in. This information may be helpful as he introduces you to others.
- Should he introduce you incorrectly, correct his mistake as soon as possible. For example, if your correct title is "Assistant Director of Marketing" and you are introduced as the "Director of Marketing," interject with the correction as soon as the mistake is made.
- Once you have been introduced, follow the tips provided in the previous sections, "*When Standing*" and "*When Sitting.*"

Introducing Others

When engaged in a conversation and someone you know joins in the conversation, it is your responsibility to introduce him to the people you are conversing with. Be sure to keep the following tips in mind as you introduce others.

- When more than one person needs to be introduced, it is proper to introduce them in descending order of their professional rank. For example, introduce the President first, then the Vice President, then the Directors and so on.

- Always introduce others by their full name and title as this example shows. "This is Mr. Robert Smith, President of XYZ Company." If Mr. Smith wishes the other person to address him differently, allow him to inform the person otherwise.
- Help the person that is joining the conversation feel welcomed by including him in the conversation. This can be accomplished by offering an additional piece of information about the person whom you are introducing. The information you offer should be of interest to all parties involved. For example, if you are aware that both parties are avid golfers, inform them of this fact. If you are not aware of a common interest, you can also inform the person joining the conversation about the topic of your discussion and ask him a question relevant to that topic.

Introduction Tools
There are a number of tools that can be used to assist with the introduction process. However, the most common tools are business cards and nametags. Following are tips and suggestions on how to use each of these tools properly to ensure a great introduction.

Business Cards
Business cards serve one primary purpose, to provide personal information about a person. Because of their importance, business cards should be cared for and exchanged in a manner that reflects their importance. Below are a few tips to keep in mind as you offer and receive business cards.
- Be sure your business cards contain up-to-date information and are clean and free of any defects. Avoid writing on your business cards to correct information. Remember, your business card is a reflection of you and should have a professional appearance.
- Store your business cards in a professional carrying case to protect them from damage.
- Always have a sufficient amount of business cards available. If you believe you may need more business cards than your carrying case will hold, consider storing additional cards in a briefcase.
- Exchange business cards during the introduction process. However, if your introduction is occurring during a meal or other function where it is not convenient to exchange business cards, then exchanging them afterwards is appropriate.

- Present your business card with your right hand and with the card facing up. In addition, present your business card so that the other person will be able to read it without turning it around.
- When a business card is offered to you, always return the courtesy by offering yours in exchange.
- When you receive a business card, look over the content briefly and ask for clarification on any confusing information, such as the pronunciation of a difficult name. Also, to demonstrate the value of the card, place it in your carrying case. Be sure to place business cards you receive toward the back of your carrying case to avoid the mistake of offering someone else's business card to another person.
- As a sign of respect to senior management, do not offer them your business card. Always allow the higher ranking official to initiate the business card exchange process. If business cards are not exchanged at the beginning of the conversation, and the person you are visiting with has requested that you contact them at a later date, it is appropriate to request their business card.
- Writing short notes on a business card is a great way to associate important information with a specific person, particularly if you are meeting several different people in a short amount of time. However, avoid writing on business cards until the conversation has ended and the person has left your vicinity.

Nametags

Although nametags do not provide as much information about a person as a business card, they do serve several important purposes. For example, during a conversation, a nametag serves as a quick reference should you forget a person's name. In addition, nametags allow you to quickly scan the names of people at an event, which allows you to choose whom you want or need to visit with. Provided below are important tips and suggestions to keep in mind when wearing a nametag.

- Before you put on your nametag, review it to ensure that the information is correct.
- Even if other people at a function may not be wearing their nametags, be sure to wear yours. Remember, your nametag helps others remember your name.
- Place your nametag on your left side, just below your shoulder. This allows others to easily view your nametag when shaking your hand.

- After attaching your nametag, ensure that it is upright, easily viewable and securely attached.

3. DEVELOPING & MAINTAINING A CONVERSATION

Once you have properly completed the introduction, you need to develop and maintain the conversation. The following steps will assist you with this process.

Starting The Conversation

Although you have a specific goal for starting a conversation, it is important to establish a rapport between you and the person you are conversing with before accomplishing your goal. Doing so will put the other person at ease and make the conversation more comfortable. As a result, the person will be more willing to share information with you.

To start a conversation, find a topic that is interesting to both of you. Finding this common interest may take a little time, particularly if you do not know the person. However, by finding a common interest, the conversation will be much easier to maintain. This section provides a few examples of questions to ask the other person when starting a conversation.

- What country, state or city is the person from? If you are familiar with that area, ask him specific questions about the area.
- What organization does the person work for and what is his role in the organization? If you are not familiar with the organization, ask him specific questions about what the organization does.
- Where did the person attend college and what did he study?

In most cases, your initial question will generate a number of additional questions that will assist in continuing the conversation. However, if the person you are talking to does not appear interested in the topic being discussed, present another topic for discussion.

Showing Interest In The Conversation

To help the person you are speaking with feel comfortable, it is essential that you show interest in the conversation. This can sometimes be difficult, particularly if the person is discussing a topic you are not interested in, or if there are distracting activities occurring around you. The key to showing interest in the conversation is to concentrate on what is being said and provide signals that you are listening. Listed below are a few signals that you may find helpful to use. In addition, review the "Non-Verbal Communication" chapter for additional tips.

- When the other person is speaking, pick up on key comments or issues discussed. Use these comments or issues when developing additional questions to ask.
- Use positive body language as you listen to the other person speak, such as leaning forward and nodding.
- Maintain eye contact.
- Occasionally provide short confirmations, such as interjecting a quick question about an item that the person has just mentioned or provide a confirming statement like "Yes" or "I know what you mean."
- Utilize the other person's name occasionally throughout the conversation. For example, when asking a question, start with a statement such as, "So, Bob, I understand you work for XYZ Corporation."

Watching For Signals
Knowing if the person is interested in having a conversation is an important skill to develop. In most cases, the person will provide signals through his body language to let you know if he is interested or not interested in participating in a conversation. For example, does the person maintain eye contact or does he frequently look around the room? Refer to the "Non-Verbal Communication" chapter to understand what a person's voice, body language and words are telling you about his level of interest in the conversation.

If you are not sure if the person is interested, or able to engage in a conversation, the best approach is to ask him if he is interested, such as "I'm sorry, is this a bad time to talk?" If he is not interested in conversing, offer an apology and move on to someone else.

Gathering Specific Information
Once the conversation has developed, you can begin the process of gathering the specific information you need to accomplish your goal. It is best to begin with small, less threatening (or invasive) questions and move to more specific questions. As you continue to ask more informative questions, watch for signs of acceptance, concern or discomfort from the

person you are speaking with. If the person is comfortable with the conversation, he will speak freely, providing you the information that you have requested. However, if he feels uncomfortable or threatened with the conversation, he may answer your question with simple, non-detailed responses, or he may not answer your question at all. If you sense that the person you are speaking with is uncomfortable with your question, switch topics and begin the process of ending the conversation. To learn more about signs of acceptance, concern or discomfort, review the "Non-Verbal Communication" chapter.

Ending The Conversation
Knowing when to end a conversation is just as important as developing and maintaining a conversation. No one enjoys engaging in a conversation and then suddenly standing there quietly looking at each other with nothing more to say. To avoid this situation, you must maintain control of the conversation. Therefore, once you have obtained your goal for engaging in a conversation, or if the person has provided you signals of disinterest, it is time to end the conversation and move on. To properly end a conversation, follow these steps.

- Summarize the information that you discussed with the person.
- If you agreed to complete a task, such as a follow-up call, remind the person when you will complete the task.
- If you have not already done so, and it is appropriate to do so, exchange business cards.
- Thank the individual for the interesting conversation as you offer your hand for a handshake. You may find it helpful to review the "Non-Verbal Communication" chapter for tips on an effective handshake.

4. CONVERSATION ETIQUETTE
When engaging in a conversation, not only is it important to understand how to develop and maintain that conversation, but also to do so in a professional manner. Poor etiquette will destroy a conversation as well as your reputation. The following sections provide several tips and suggestions on how to conduct a conversation in a professional manner.

Dominating The Conversation

The purpose of a conversation is just that – to have a conversation. If you dominate the conversation by doing all the talking, you not only distance yourself from the other person, but also fail to gather any information. To avoid this situation, encourage the person you are speaking with to talk by asking "open-ended" questions. In addition, avoid interrupting the other person while he is speaking.

Topics And Issues To Avoid

Certain topic and issues should be avoided when conducting a conversation as they can create un-needed tension and/or disputes. The following bullet points provide a few topics and issues that should be avoided.

- Politics and religion are very personal topics and therefore should be avoided unless they are directly relevant to the reason you are engaging in the conversation. For example, discussing politics would be appropriate if your work involves representing a political candidate and you are at a function encouraging attendees to support that candidate.
- Personal issues, such as health and financial concerns, are private and should not be discussed.
- Humor, when used appropriately, is a great tool to develop a conversation. However, humor is never appropriate when it is used at someone else's expense.
- Technical or company jargon is appropriate when used in an environment where everyone is familiar with these words or phrases. However, if the person you are speaking with is not familiar with this terminology, you may cause the individual to feel uncomfortable or embarrassed.
- Negative feedback, such as putting a person down or correcting him, will only create tension in a conversation and should be avoided.
- Providing personal advice can have serious ramifications. If you find yourself engaged in a conversation where the other person is discussing a personal issue, avoid providing advice. Instead respond with supportive comments, such as, "Wow, that's too bad" or "I hope things work out for you" and try to re-direct the conversation to a new topic.

Body Language

As mentioned earlier in this chapter, people communicate in a variety of ways during a conversation. Body language plays an important role in how you communicate. Controlling and understanding your body language is essential to effectively communicating with others. To learn more about the use of body language, review the "Non-Verbal Communication" chapter.

Spoken Language

What you say, as well as how you say it, is often your most effective form of communication. Therefore, it is imperative that you speak correctly. The following bullet points provide some tips and suggestions to assist you with your spoken language.

- Having others understand what you are saying is essential to a good conversation. Be sure to take the time to speak and pronounce your words clearly.
- Listening to someone who speaks too fast or too slow can be very annoying and difficult. If you are concerned about the speed at which you speak, have a friend engage in a conversation with you and have them evaluate the speed at which you speak.
- Trendy slang words or phrases, as well as cursing, reflect poor vocabulary skills, and therefore should be avoided during professional conversations.
- Voice fluctuations are a great way to emphasize certain parts of your conversation. However, too much emphasis can be distracting.

Names

Using a person's name when you are speaking is a sign that you value conversing with that person. Forgetting or mispronouncing a person's name can be embarrassing, and can ruin the conversation. To avoid these situations, consider using some of the following tips and suggestions.

- During the introduction, repeat the person's name. For example, when meeting Robert Smith, you might say, "Hi, Robert, it is a pleasure to meet you."
- If you did not hear the person's name, politely ask him to repeat it.
- To help remember a person's name, repeat the name several times in your head or try associating the person's name with an object they are wearing. For example, if Robert Smith is wearing a red shirt, think to yourself "Robert, red shirt." In addition, using the person's name

throughout the conversation is a great way to remember the other person's name.

- When talking to someone that you had been introduced to at a previous engagement, but you are not sure if the individual remembers your name, offer your name again and remind the individual where you had previously met.
- If you have difficulty remembering names, apologize and request the person's name again.
- When introduced to a person with a name that is difficult to pronounce, repeat the person's name and ask him if you pronounced it correctly.
- If your name is difficult to pronounce, offer assistance in how your name is pronounced, such as saying your name slowly or offering words that sound similar to your name.

Group Conversations

When engaged in a group conversation, many of the same skills and issues discussed in this chapter are applicable to a group conversation. However, one issue of importance in a group conversation is making sure that everyone in the group has the ability to participate in the conversation. As you can imagine, the more people involved in a group discussion, the harder the task becomes. However, as you begin to develop the skills and tips provided throughout this chapter, conducting an effective group conversation will become easier.

Trust And Confidence

Occasionally you may be exposed to a conversation where personal or confidential information is discussed in trust. Maintaining this trust is not only important in developing a strong relationship, but also maintaining a reputation as a trustworthy person. If you are provided with personal or confidential information, avoid discussing the topics of these conversations with others.

5. DEVELOPING CONVERSATION SKILLS

Becoming an effective conversationalist will not happen overnight. Like most skills, to be good at it, you need to practice. To develop your skills, consider implementing some of the following tips and suggestions.

- Encourage coworkers or friends to engage in conversations with you.

- Videotape yourself having a conversation with someone and review the videotape for areas where you need improvement.
- Enroll in a public speaking course.
- Attend functions, such as industry luncheons, trade shows or business meetings, where you can practice your conversation skills.
- Consider meeting with a speech therapist if you are having difficulty developing your skills.
- Join a club or professional organization that allows you to meet new people as well as develop your conversation skills.
- Read a variety of literature on developing your conversation and public speaking skills. No matter how well you believe your conversation skills are, there is no harm in learning new techniques.

MANAGING & PARTICIPATING IN A BUSINESS MEETING

A business meeting is a communication device used to open the lines of communication among different departments within an organization or between different organizations. The primary functions of a business meeting are to discuss strategies, present proposals, and plan upcoming activities. Some organizations conduct business meetings on a regular basis, while others may only do so occasionally. Chances are that you will be asked to participate, and even manage, several business meetings during your career. This chapter provides helpful tips and suggestions on how to successfully manage and participate in a business meeting.

1. PREPARING FOR A BUSINESS MEETING

The key to a successful business meeting is preparation. Whether you are managing a business meeting or participating in it, everyone has a role in the preparation. This section provides tips and suggestions to consider as the manager or a participant of a business meeting.

Meeting Manager
- Define the reason for a meeting, as well as the goal you want to accomplish by having a meeting.
- Consider the format of your meeting. For instance, will the meeting be structured so you are able to maintain complete control or will it be informal and free flowing to encourage participants to brainstorm?

- Carefully choose your participants to include those people that will add value to the meeting and possibly those that may be affected by the outcome of the meeting.
- Create two agendas for your meeting. One agenda is for you and should include items that you wish to discuss, as well as the estimated time to complete the different segments of the meeting. The second agenda is created for the participants and should include the date of the meeting, time and agenda, as well as assignments you wish the participants to complete prior to the meeting.
- Ensure participants attend your meeting by sending out a reminder e-mail or a note a few days before the meeting. In addition, you may find it helpful to contact your participants by telephone.
- Have extra copies of the meeting agenda available in case your participants forget to bring theirs with them. In addition, if you are conducting a follow-up meeting, be sure to bring reports from previous meetings with you in case you need to refer to them.
- Arrange for a person to take minutes during the meeting to allow you to focus your attention on the meeting.
- At least an hour before your meeting is scheduled to begin, check out your meeting facilities to ensure everything is organized and arranged as you have requested.

Meeting Participant
- Respond to an invitation to participate in a business meeting as soon as possible. If you are unable to attend the meeting, inform the meeting manager of your prior obligation and request that the meeting minutes be forwarded to you. However, if you are able to attend, but anticipate that you will be arriving late, be sure to inform the meeting manager of your situation.
- Review the meeting agenda and complete any assignments prior to the meeting. If you did not receive an agenda, request that the meeting manager provide you one.
- Bring your agenda, materials from previous meetings, as well as any other related materials to the meeting.

2. CONDUCTING A BUSINESS MEETING
When managing a business meeting, it is your responsibility to control how the meeting is conducted. Maintaining this control will allow you to not

only accomplish your goals, but also to do so in a timely fashion. This section provides several tips and suggestions on how to maintain control of your meeting.

- Start the meeting on time. Starting late creates frustration among the participants and can be perceived by the participants as your inability to organize a meeting.
- If you must start the meeting late, for example, if a significant number of your participants are running late, inform the other participants why the meeting is not starting on time and consider conducting an activity that will fill the wait time, such as performing introductions.
- Be sure all of the participants know one another. Introductions can be conducted individually before the start of the meeting or conducted as a group at the beginning of the meeting.
- Avoid delaying your meeting by stopping your presentation to provide quick summaries of the meeting to participants that arrive late. Simply continue with the meeting and during the next break provide those participants any information they may need.
- Stick to your agenda. If participants are spending too much time on a specific topic or issue, or if they are not addressing the correct topic or issue at hand, stop whatever discussions are occurring, get the participants to refocus their attention, and continue the meeting. You may find it helpful to provide the participants hints or guides, such as starting them off on the right track or giving them a few answers.
- Be sure that all attendees participate, and that everyone's opinion is heard. Doing so will add diversity to the conversation and build trust between you and the participants.
- Observe the non-verbal communication signals of your participants. If you notice that your participants appear confused or bored, stop and ask for questions or reevaluate how you should continue the discussion to regain the participants' attention. You may find it helpful to review the "Non Verbal Communication" chapter for additional information on determining the level of a person's interest.
- When specific questions need to be answered as part of the meeting, avoid accepting answers derived from a group consensus. Group consensus is a situation when a few dominant participants coerce other participants into agreeing with their answer just to get the task

completed, even though the other participants may not necessarily agree that the other participant's answer is the best option. To avoid a group consensus, consider requesting that all of the participants provide separate answers and then evaluate all the suggestions as a group.

3. PARTICIPATING IN A BUSINESS MEETING

As the participant of a business meeting, your role is to provide value to the meeting. This value is not only in what you have to say, but also in what you have to do at the meeting. Provided below are some tips on how to be a valuable participant of a business meeting.

- Arrive at the meeting on time. If you arrive late, join the meeting as discreetly as possible without bringing attention to yourself. After the meeting is completed, be sure to apologize to the meeting manager for your tardiness.
- Allow the meeting manager to conduct the meeting. Remember, you were invited to the meeting to participate, not to co-manage.
- Participate when you believe you have something of value to add to the meeting. Avoid participating solely as a method to let yourself be heard or to appear as if you are important.
- Always ask questions if you are unsure of an issue or topic being discussed or if you need to have information clarified.
- Do not be embarrassed to get involved. Remember that you were invited to participate in the meeting because the meeting manager believes you can add value to the discussion.
- Avoid being disruptive, such as conducting unrelated conversations with other participants, not paying attention, or showing signs of lack of interest.
- Take notes on topics, issues or questions discussed during the meeting to help you stay focused on the meeting. However, do not become so engrossed in taking notes that you are not able to participate.

4. ENDING A BUSINESS MEETING

Ending a business meeting is the responsibility of the meeting manager. As with conducting the meeting, ending a meeting must be controlled properly. This will ensure that all participants have an adequate opportunity to ask questions and that they are aware of any assignments they need to complete, as well as the time frame in which they need to be completed. This section provides several tips and suggestions on ensuring that these tasks, and others, are successfully completed at the end of a business meeting.

- Leave adequate time to wrap up the meeting. The more details discussed during the meeting, the more time that should be allowed for questions.
- Allow participants an opportunity to ask questions.
- Summarize the results of the meeting, discuss an action plan, provide assignments and deadlines, and discuss when any follow-up items, such as another meeting, must be conducted.
- Request and answer any additional questions related to the content of the meeting or the follow-up items.
- Thank the participants for their time and valuable input.

5. FOLLOWING-UP ON A BUSINESS MEETING

The final component of a business meeting is the follow-up. This is the last opportunity for everyone that was involved in the meeting to review the materials presented during the meeting, provide additional comments or ask any final questions. Although the responsibility of conducting the follow-up falls on the meeting manager, participants do have some follow-up responsibilities as well. This section provides a few suggestions to keep in mind when conducting the follow-up for a business meeting.

Meeting Manager

- Distribute meeting minutes from the meeting to all the participants within one or two business days of concluding the meeting. Establish a deadline for when participants can provide you additional information and comments to be included in the final meeting minutes.
- Remind participants that agreed to complete specific assignments when their assignments are to be completed. You may find it helpful to personally contact these participants to ensure that their assignments will be completed on time.
- Evaluate the success of your business meeting and the areas that may need improvement. You may find it helpful to contact a few participants of your business meeting and request that they evaluate your performance.

Meeting Participant

- Review the meeting minutes as soon as possible to avoid forgetting information that was presented at the meeting. If you wish to add additional information to the minutes, or you have a question about the content, contact the meeting manager as soon as possible.
- Complete any assignments that you agreed to conduct as soon as possible. If you have any questions about your assignment, contact your meeting manager for assistance.
- Keep the meeting manager informed of your progress on any assignment that you have been assigned, as well as the estimated completion date.

MENTORS

A mentor is an experienced and trusted advisor, such as a person with a specialized skill or a person that is successful in his profession. In addition to his knowledge, a good mentor also has the ability to teach, is trustworthy, and is willing to assist others. Having a great mentor can be a career enriching experience. Therefore, it is important that you take the time and effort to choose a mentor that will best meet your needs. This chapter will not only look into the benefits of having a great mentor, but also what qualities to look for in a mentor, how to select a mentor, as well as how to develop a positive relationship with your mentor.

1. WHY HAVE A MENTOR?

There are numerous reasons why you should develop a relationship with a mentor. Below are just a few of these reasons.

- A mentor can help you understand the makeup of your organization and how best to use your skills to maximize your potential within the organization.
- A mentor can assist you in keeping your professional problems in perspective, as well as teach you how to strategize and develop plans to handle them.
- A mentor can provide honest feedback and helpful criticism.
- A mentor can assist you in developing professional contacts, as well as provide suggestions on how to network within your industry.
- A mentor can provide advice on how to accomplish your career goals.

2. QUALITIES TO LOOK FOR IN A MENTOR

Locating the most suitable mentor takes time and research. Just because a person is successful in his career does not necessarily mean that he has the skills or is capable of being a good mentor. Therefore, develop a list of qualities you are looking for in a mentor and use this list to evaluate potential candidates. The following qualities may be helpful as a guide in developing your list.

- Someone that you admire and that is well respected within your organization or the industry in which you work.
- Someone that has successfully mentored, or is currently mentoring other people that have similar skills, goals or background as you.
- Someone that has skills or knowledge that you value or wish to develop.
- Someone that you can relate to. For example, someone with a similar social or educational background as you.
- Someone that is a good listener.
- Someone that is familiar with your position and the projects you will be working on.
- Someone that is capable to meet with you on a regular basis and is willing to take the time to assist you.

3. SELECTING A MENTOR

Selecting a mentor is almost equivalent to participating in a job interview. Not only are you telling the potential mentor why you want him to be your mentor, but also why he should invest his time in becoming your mentor. This section provides several helpful tips and suggestions to consider when selecting a mentor.

- Once you have developed a list of qualities that you are looking for in a mentor (*see the previous section*), develop a list of qualified candidates and rank them beginning with the most qualified.
- Qualified candidates can include a supervisor or manager within your organization, a friend, an acquaintance from a professional association, a past professor, or even a previous employer.
- Develop a letter to your potential mentor explaining your reason for writing, why you believe that person would be a great mentor, the benefits such a relationship would provide for you, as well as the benefits the potential mentor would gain by becoming your mentor. Be sure to

also include the time requirements that you foresee the relationship encompassing. If you are closely associated with the potential mentor, you may choose to contact him directly about your proposal versus contacting him through a letter.

- Be sure to provide the potential mentor your current resume in order for him to evaluate your professional background.

- Follow-up your letter with a request to meet and discuss your proposal for a mentoring relationship. If the person is hesitant about becoming a mentor, inform him that you would enjoy the opportunity to meet with him and to discuss the proposal further. Then, at that time, if he decides that he is not able or willing to be your mentor, request if he can recommend someone else that would be a qualified mentor for you.

- Some organizations provide their employees with internal mentors. These can be pre-selected for you, or you may be able to choose a mentor from a pre-selected group of candidates. Although a pre-selected mentor may be capable of meeting your needs and have the qualities that you are looking for, discussing internal organizational problems or conflicts with a fellow employee can be uncomfortable. If so, consider developing an additional mentoring relationship with someone outside of your company.

- Never pressure someone into becoming a mentor. Remember, a mentor should be someone that is capable and willing to help you. Someone that is pressured into becoming a mentor may not be as dedicated to the relationship as you had hoped they would be.

4. DEVELOPING A RELATIONSHIP WITH YOUR MENTOR

When you have established a relationship with a mentor, you need to take the appropriate steps to develop that relationship. This section provides several tips and suggestions to help you develop a positive relationship with your mentor.

- Respect your mentor's time. Schedule regular meetings, such as once every month or two. Avoid scheduling meetings too frequently as the relationship may become too demanding for the mentor. In addition, always arrive to your meetings on time. Should you need to contact your mentor outside of a scheduled meeting, do so through e-mail or a short telephone call.

- Be prepared for your meetings. Although it is a good idea to use a few of the meetings to learn a little bit more about each other, avoid using the entire meeting for this purpose, and always have professional issues available to discuss.
- Always keep the relationship with your mentor professional. Therefore, maintain professionalism during your meetings and avoid discussing personal matters.
- When requesting assistance or feedback from your mentor, be open-minded to his advice, suggestions or criticism. Also, be sure to provide your mentor updates on any feedback that he has provided you in the past.
- After each meeting, send a card or e-mail to your mentor thanking him for his time and assistance. In addition, offer to conduct your meetings over a meal and pick up the tab as a token of your appreciation. If your mentor happens to work at your company, consider carbon copying your thank you letter or e-mail to your mentor's supervisor.
- Avoid letting your mentoring relationship stagnate. If your schedule becomes too busy to maintain the relationship, inform your mentor about the situation and discuss alternative meeting times or other communication options that will allow you to continue the relationship.

NETWORKING

You are probably familiar with the phrase "It's not what you know, but who you know." Having a good education and knowing how to do your job successfully are obviously an important part of your career. However, to be successful in your career, you must learn to network like a professional. This chapter will not only explain why networking is such an essential part of your career, but also describes how to develop a network of contacts that will assist you in your career.

1. WHAT IS NETWORKING & WHY IS IT IMPORTANT?

Networking is a term commonly used to refer to the act of creating personal and professional relationships for the purpose of exchanging information, advice, contacts, or support. As you can imagine, all of these factors play an important role in the success of your career. To give you an example of why networking is important, consider the following example.

Example:
Bill Backpack is currently the Director of Advertising at XYZ, Inc. He has become aware from an acquaintance at WeKnowThings, LLC that ABC Corp. is currently considering implementing a multi-million dollar advertising program for their new widget. Bill wants to be part of ABC Corp.'s contract. Therefore, he asks his acquaintance at WeKnowThings, LLC to introduce him to his contact at ABC Corp. by setting up a lunch meeting.

At the lunch meeting, Bill is introduced to Melissa from ABC Corp. Bill learns from Melissa that ABC Corp. is targeting publications for their new advertising program that will reach readers between the ages of 25-40. Bill informs Melissa that his company specifically targets that market and would love to have the opportunity to discuss how his company can assist them with the promotion of their widget. Melissa is excited about the opportunity and invites Bill to meet with her and her boss to discuss the potential relationship.

Later that week, Bill meets with Melissa and her boss. They like the proposal Bill presents and they award Bill a $1.3 million advertising program.

As you can see from this example, networking can be an extremely valuable tool when used properly.

2. BUILDING AN EFFECTIVE NETWORK

Building an effective network of contacts involves determining who can assist you, finding out what information these people have to offer you, and understanding where to find a network of contacts. To build an effective network that will provide you the most benefits, be sure to consider the following tips and suggestions.

Determine Who Can Assist You

The key to developing an effective network is developing relationships with people who have access to the information you need. However, never underestimate the value of potential relationships. For example, you might believe developing a relationship with your supervisor's assistant may not be worth your time, yet this person usually has access to a wealth of information, such as when important meetings are taking place or when is the best time to approach your supervisor about requesting vacation time. Therefore, as you meet new people, be sure to take the time to understand what that person's roles and responsibilities are, and determine how they might be able to assist you in the future.

Inform Others Of The Value You Have To Offer

When developing a relationship with a new contact, always be sure to inform that person about the information you have access to that can be of assistance to them. By making yourself more valuable to others, the more valuable they potentially become to you. For example, say you are trying to develop a relationship with the new Director of Advertising at XYZ, Inc.

You know from your research this person enjoys writing novels as a hobby. During your conversation, you inform him that you also enjoy writing and are currently presiding as President of a local writers group and that you would be happy to introduce him to some of the other authors, editors and printers in the area. By informing him of the value that you have to offer (access to local authors, editors and printers), he will be more willing to share information about potential advertising opportunities that may exist within his organization or other organizations.

Develop Contacts Within Your Own Organization and Industry

Developing contacts within your own organization and industry provides you the ability to be aware of potential threats and opportunities that can affect you and your organization. The best method to develop these contacts is to become an active participant in organizational events and industry groups. For example, offer to be part of a multi-department team at work or become an active participant in an industry trade group or association. Another method to develop contacts within your industry, and have access to new up-and-coming professionals, is to become an active participant in your college or universities' Career Service Department. By assisting soon-to-be or recent graduates with getting started in your industry, these students are likely become allies, as well as valuable resources of information as they continue to grow in their careers.

Develop Contacts Outside Of Your Industry

Many people make the mistake of networking solely within their own organization or industry. Although these contacts are important, limiting the spectrum of your contacts also limits your access to new opportunities. Therefore, consider becoming an active participant with groups outside of your industry, such as your college or universities' Alumni Association or a young professionals' group.

3. NETWORKING TIPS

As described throughout this chapter, networking is an important part of developing a successful career. Therefore, before you start to actively build your network of contacts, be sure to consider some of these tips.

- You may find it helpful to review the "Introductions & Conversations" chapter. Many of the same skills discussed in that chapter directly relate to the networking process.

- As you build your network of contacts, develop a system to keep track of your network of contacts, such as who the people are, what their contact information is, and a note about how they can assist you.

- Stay in touch with your network of contacts. However, avoid contacting them only when you are looking for information or assistance as this can cause you to develop a reputation as someone who only cares about what you want. Instead, develop a "win-win" relationship. For example, call to inform your contact about a recent article you read in an industry publication that he might find interesting. By calling to offer information, the more likely that person will call you when he comes across information that he believes will be helpful to you.

- Practice your skills. The more you practice your networking skills, the more effective you will become. Therefore, attend various functions, and practice your skills. You may even find it helpful to have a friend watch you as you practice networking to offer you advice on how to develop your skills further.

NON-VERBAL COMMUNICATION

Communicating effectively is an important part of a successful career. Yet many people make the mistake of focusing their efforts on developing their verbal communication skills and not enough time on their non-verbal communication skills. This chapter will highlight important forms of non-verbal communication, as well as how to use them effectively.

1. THE HANDSHAKE

An important form of non-verbal communication used frequently in the business world is the handshake. Because the handshake is often the first contact made between two people, it is important that it be executed correctly to develop a positive first impression.

When Is A Handshake Appropriate

Although a handshake can generate positive responses when executed correctly, there are some situations when a handshake is not appropriate. Provided below are a few examples of when a handshake is appropriate.

- When you are being introduced or are meeting someone for the first time, such as at a business luncheon or seminar.
- When meeting or visiting with someone you have not seen for an extended period of time.
- When congratulating another person.
- When saying goodbye to someone that you may not see again for an extended period of time.

Preparing For A Handshake

The first step to a successful handshake is being prepared. If you are in an environment where you know you will be performing a handshake, consider the following advice.

- Be sure your hand will be comfortable for the other person to shake. For example, if your hand is cold or clammy, consider inconspicuously placing your hand in your pants' pocket, holding a napkin, or rubbing your hands together to warm them up or to dry them off.
- If you are carrying items in your right hand, such as food, a drink, or a briefcase, carry these items in your left hand or set them down.
- Determine if the person you anticipate shaking hands with is able to shake your hand. For example, if the person's right hand/arm is physically handicapped, or if they are holding food or a drink, it may be uncomfortable or impossible for them to shake your hand. If you are concerned that the person may not be able to shake your hand, simply allow them to initiate the handshake.

Performing The Handshake

When performing a handshake, do so with confidence and ease. The following steps will assist you in performing a handshake successfully.

- Make eye contact with the person you will be shaking hands with, smile, and extend your right hand confidently.
- As you extend your right hand, briefly look to the other person's hand and firmly grasp their full hand so that the web between your thumb and forefinger is touching the other person's web.
- Maintain eye contact, lean forward slightly, and shake their hand two or three times at the most.
- After the second or third shake, release your grasp of the person's hand and place your hand to your side.

Handling A "Non-Responsive" Handshake Offer

Occasionally you will encounter a situation where you offer your hand for a handshake and the other person does not offer their hand in return. This usually occurs because the other person is physically unable to shake your hand or he did not notice your hand being offered. Although this is an uncomfortable situation, you can minimize your embarrassment and the embarrassment of the other person by following these steps.

- If the other person is physically unable to perform a handshake and you have offered him your hand, acknowledge your mistake. However, do not dwell on the mistake. Instead, offer an apology, such as "I'm sorry," and maintain eye contact as you return your hand to your side and continue your introduction.
- If the other person did not notice that you have offered your hand for a handshake, do not apologize. Apologizing will only cause the other person to become embarrassed. Instead, subtly return your hand to your side and continue your introduction.

2. POSTURE

How a person stands, sits or walks says a lot about that person. Even though posture plays an important role in the perception that others have of people, rarely do we spend the time to review or develop this skill. This section will provide suggestions and tips on how to use your posture when standing, sitting and walking to exude a sense of confidence and professionalism.

Your Posture While Standing

While standing, it is important to appear confident and professional. However, it is also important to do so in a manner that is comfortable to maintain, particularly if you will be standing for an extended period of time. The proper posture when standing is to stand tall with your back straight, chest out, shoulders pulled back, and arms to your sides. You may find it helpful to practice your standing posture in front of a mirror to find the posture that best fits your needs. In addition, the following tips may be of assistance.

- When entering an environment where other people are gathered, take a moment to think about your posture and what you would like your posture to tell others about you. Doing so will cause you to become more conscious of your posture.
- Avoid locking your knees and standing straight up and down. Instead, occasionally shift your weight from one leg to the other by bending one knee. You may find it helpful to practice various stances in front of a mirror to develop one that is both comfortable and professional looking.

- While speaking with another person, lean towards that person. This will give the individual the perception that you are interested in what is being said.
- Avoid crossing your arms in front of you or clasping your hands together in front of or behind your body, as this can jeopardize your posture.
- If you have difficulty keeping your arms to your sides, consider grasping an object in one hand, such as a pen. This simple task serves as a reminder to keep your arms to your sides and provides a simple form of security.
- Avoid leaning against or on objects, such as a wall or chair. This can jeopardize your posture and can be perceived by others as a sign that you are tired or bored.

Your Posture While Sitting
Although sitting is a form of relaxation, it is important to maintain proper posture, particularly when other people are present. The following points will assist you in developing a professional posture when sitting.

- When in the process of sitting, avoid "plopping" down in the chair. Instead, stand directly in front of the chair, place your hands on the arms of the chair, and lower yourself into the sitting position.
- Maintain the same upper body position as mentioned in the previous section, and allow your back to rest against the back of the chair.
- If the chair in which you are sitting has arms, rest your arms on them. Otherwise, rest your arms on your legs.
- When in a serious environment, keep both feet on the floor. If the environment is more relaxed and space allows, crossing your legs may be appropriate. However, this should only be done if you will not jeopardize your posture. You may find it helpful to sit in front of a mirror while crossing your legs to determine how this position affects your posture.

Your Posture While Walking
While walking, you should maintain the same posture as discussed in the "Your Posture While Standing" section. In addition, the following points will provide you tips on maintaining a confident, professional appearance as you walk.

- Walk with your head high and chin tucked in. Avoid holding your chin up, as this is a sign of pride and gives the appearance that you are unapproachable.
- Move with purpose and direction. This will provide others the sense that you are alert and aware.
- While at work, walk at a faster than normal pace. This projects an image that you are actively attending to your work.

3. PROFESSIONAL ATTIRE

As with other forms of non-verbal communication, your choice of attire sends a strong message to others about the type of person you are. For more information about professional attire, review the "Professional Attire" chapter.

4. FACIAL EXPRESSIONS

Facial expressions are a powerful form of non-verbal communication. They provide obvious signs of a person's interest level, understanding and confidence. Provided below are tips and suggestions on how to use your facial expressions to communicate with others.

- Look others in the eye when communicating. However, avoid maintaining continuous eye contact, as this can become uncomfortable for you and the person you are speaking with.
- If you are uncomfortable looking someone directly in the eye, focus on the area between the other person's eyes. However, avoid focusing on other areas of the person's face, as this can cause a person to become self-conscious.
- Avoid looking at other people or activities occurring around you as you converse with another person. Doing so is disrespectful and a sign to the other person that you are uninterested in the conversation.
- Smile regularly. Smiling sends a message to others that you are approachable, confident, and interested in the other person.
- Practice your facial expressions to ensure that you are sending the correct message to others. For example, stand in front of a mirror and practice the facial expression you would use if the person you were visiting with just told you something interesting, shocking or depressing.

5. GESTURES

Using gestures, such as hand movements or facial expressions, is an effective method of communicating. When used correctly, gestures can enhance a conversation by emphasizing certain points. However, if used incorrectly, gestures can become annoying and/or even cause others to become distracted. The following points will provide suggestions on how to effectively use and develop your gestures.

- Try to keep your gestures smooth and flowing. Sudden movements can cause listeners to become distracted.
- Vary the gestures you use and avoid using certain gestures too frequently as this can cause your gestures to lose their effectiveness.
- It is important to practice your gestures on other people to determine how others will interpret your gestures. Therefore, practice using various gestures with a friend or colleague, and ask them to provide you feedback.

6. DISTANCE & SPACE

Distance and space are important factors to be aware of as you interact with others. If people feel that you are invading their personal space, they may become uncomfortable and/or defensive. Below are some tips and suggestions to keep in mind as you interact with others.

- In the United States it is customary to maintain a distance of at least three to four feet between yourself and the person with whom you are speaking.
- Be aware that the space requirement among other cultures may be increased or decreased. If you will be traveling outside of the United States to conduct business, or you will be conducting business with people from another culture, consider purchasing professional travel guides to gather specific information regarding the business customs of that culture.
- When in an environment where maintaining an appropriate distance is not possible, such as a crowded room, adjust your distance accordingly.
- Always knock before entering another person's office regardless if the door is open or closed, as a sign of respect. When entering another person's office, wait to be seated until you are invited to do so.

- If the person you want to visit with is on the telephone, avoid waiting in the immediate area until the individual is finished. Instead, return in a few minutes, leave a note with their assistant, or send an e-mail informing the individual that you wish to visit with him when he is available. In addition, if you are engaged in a conversation and the other person receives a telephone call, offer to excuse yourself.
- When conversing with a person that is seated, place yourself in a position where you can maintain eye contact with that person.

OFFICE ETIQUETTE: EQUIPMENT, SUPPLIES & COMMON AREAS

Every office contains equipment, supplies and common areas that are shared by multiple people. Unlike personal items, shared items require additional care and attention to maximize their performance or service. Therefore, it is important that you do your part to care for these items. If not, you run the risk of developing a reputation among your colleagues as being disrespectful or inconsiderate. This chapter focuses on commonly shared items and spaces in a business office and provides tips on the proper etiquette and care for each.

1. THE FAX MACHINE

The fax machine is one of the most commonly used communication devices in an office. In fact, it is not uncommon for a fax machine in a busy office to process hundreds of documents each day. Because of the importance of the fax machine, it is imperative that it be cared for regularly. Listed below are some tips to keep in mind when using the fax machine. In addition, you may find it helpful to review the "Faxes" section in the "Electronic Communication" chapter.

- Unless absolutely necessary, avoid sending lengthy faxes during peak usage hours. Instead, consider sending longer faxes first thing in the morning, during lunch hours, or at the end of the day.
- As faxes arrive, are sent, or when confirmation reports are generated, do not leave them on or around the fax. If you notice faxes or confirmation

reports gathering on or around the fax machine, deliver them to the correct person or place them in the appropriate person's mailbox.

- When sorting documents processed by the fax machine, organize the documents in their correct order. You may find it helpful to paperclip or staple the pages of a document together to avoid losing or misplacing part of the document.
- If the fax machine is not working properly, attempt to fix it. If you are unable to correct the problem, inform the appropriate person. In addition, leave a note on the fax machine or send an e-mail informing your colleagues of the situation.
- If your fax machine requires departmental authorization codes, be sure to use the appropriate codes.
- Avoid using the fax machine for personal items. If circumstances arise that require personal use of the fax machine, request approval from your supervisor before proceeding.

2. THE PRINTER

Of all the equipment in an office, the shared office printer is often the most utilized. Because of the large volume of paper being processed by the printer, as well as the number of people using the printer, it is important that the printer be cared for to avoid back-ups, breakdowns and lost documents. Listed below are a few important tips to keep in mind should you need to use a shared printer.

- Avoid printing lengthy documents or completing specialized printings during peak usage hours. Instead, consider printing longer documents first thing in the morning, during lunch hours, or at the end of the day. If you must print a document that may delay other print jobs, inform your colleagues before sending the document to the printer to allow them the opportunity to print their documents first.
- After completing a large print job, or completing several smaller jobs, check the printer to determine if additional paper is needed.
- Pick up documents as soon as they are printed. If another person's documents are gathering on or around the printer, take the documents to the person or place them in the person's mailbox.
- If the printer is not working properly, attempt to fix it. If you are unable to correct the problem, inform the appropriate person. In addition, leave

a note on the printer or send an e-mail informing your colleagues of the situation.

- Avoid using the printer to print personal items. If circumstances arise that require personal use of the printer, request approval from your supervisor before proceeding.
- If you change the type of paper in the printer trays, make sure that you change the paper back to the previous type so that the next user is not inconvenienced.

3. THE COPIER

Of all the equipment in an office, the copier tends to be the one piece of equipment that can cause the most tension among co-workers. Avoid this tension by following these recommendations.

- As with other shared equipment, avoid copying large documents or processing detailed jobs during peak usage hours. Instead, consider copying first thing in the morning, during lunch hours, or at the end of the day. If you need to use the copier for an extended amount of time, inform your colleagues before starting the job to allow them the opportunity to copy their documents first.
- If you are conducting a large copying job and a colleague needs to use the copier, offer to interrupt your job or to copy his job for him once you are finished.
- If you notice the paper trays are low, or you have just completed a large print job, always refill the trays prior to leaving the copier.
- Avoid leaving the copier when conducting a copy job in case the copier jams or the copier finishes before you return.
- Should a colleague leave documents in or around the copier, deliver them to the appropriate person or place them in the person's mailbox.
- If the copier jams or is not printing correctly, attempt to fix it. If you are unable to correct the problem, inform the appropriate person. In addition, leave a note on the copier or send an e-mail informing your colleagues of the situation.
- If your copier requires departmental authorization codes, use the appropriate codes for your copy job. If a colleague has left the copier before clearing the code from the machine, clear it and proceed with your job using your own authorization code.

- Avoid using the copier to copy personal items. If circumstances arise that require personal use of the copier, request approval from your supervisor before proceeding.

4. OFFICE SUPPLIES

Most offices contain an area where supplies are stored, such as a supply closet or room. In order for the supply area to work properly, it is important that it be monitored and cared for regularly. This section provides several tips and suggestions to keep in mind when using office supplies.

- When taking supplies from the supply area, only take the amount of supplies you need. If you notice certain supplies have been depleted or will need to be ordered soon, inform the appropriate person of the situation so additional supplies can be ordered.
- If you require a large amount of supplies to complete a project, inform the person in charge of the supply area about your needs. This will ensure that enough supplies will be available for you and your colleagues.
- Avoid using office supplies for personal use. If a situation arises that requires personal use of office supplies, seek approval from your supervisor before proceeding.

5. COMMON AREAS

Most companies provide their employees common areas, such as a kitchenette or break room to eat and relax. Because all employees share these areas, maintenance is everyone's responsibility. Below are some tips to keep in mind when using these facilities.

- Always clean up after yourself and put items away after you are done using them. If you notice that your colleagues have left items out, or have forgotten to take items with them after they have left, put the items away or return the items to them.
- Avoid using too much space in the cupboards or refrigerator to store your personal items. If space is limited, consider storing additional items in your office.
- Remove or throw away items that you no longer need to avoid spoilage and using too much space.

- If your office provides coffee or water service, make a new batch of coffee or replace the water jug if you notice they are empty or if you take the last serving.
- When preparing food at work, be conscious of the smell the food will generate. If the smell will be overwhelming, avoid preparing such foods in the office.
- Never use or take items that do not belong to you. If you wish to use someone else's items, always request permission first. However, do not make a habit of such requests.

OFFICE POLITICS

Politics is defined as the art and science of using opinions, policies and procedures to participate in a governing system. In the business world, the governing system is the organization that you work for, and you and your colleagues are the politicians. As a politician, you must learn how to use the opinions of your colleagues, as well as the policies and procedures of the organization, to your advantage. In order to do this, you need to gather information about how your organization operates, determine "who's who" in your organization, as well as understand your role within the organization. The more information you have, the more powerful you become. This chapter describes how to obtain this information and how to use it to your advantage.

1. KNOW HOW YOUR ORGANIZATION OPERATES

An important component of being politically savvy includes knowing how your organization operates. By understanding how your organization operates, you will be able to perform your job in a manner that will enable you to avoid possible problems and conflicts with your colleagues. In addition, it will assist you to position yourself for advancement within the organization. The following bullet points highlight important information about your organization that you should know.

- Determine what the organization's corporate culture is. For example, is the corporate culture relaxed, professional, or casual? The corporate culture usually originates from top management through the policies and procedures that they implement, as well as the actions that they take. Examples include your organization's dress code and marketing programs.

- Know the history, as well as the future plans of the organization. Examples include how did the organization get started, what has contributed to key successes, and what are the organization's long-term plans?

- Familiarize yourself with the products and services offered by your organization, such as who purchases them, how they are used, and how your organization's products and services compare to those offered by competing organizations.

- Learn the policies and procedures of your organization. These are usually outlined in your employee handbook. In addition, information regarding an organization's policies and procedures can be obtained from the Human Resource Department.

- Determine the financial viability of the organization. This type of information can usually be obtained from the organization's annual report.

2. KNOW "WHO'S WHO" IN YOUR ORGANIZATION

"It's not what you know, but who you know." This phrase is synonymous with success in office politics. By determining who can help or hurt you within your organization, you can associate yourself with the "right people." These people will not only help you avoid possible conflicts, but also help you position yourself as one of the "right people." The following tips and suggestions will assist you in determining "who's who" within your organization.

- Determine the chain of command between you and the top of the organizational chart. Once you have determined the chain of command, contact those people periodically so that they are familiar with you, as well as the contributions that you are making to the organization.

- Develop a communication network within the organization. Your communication network should include people at various levels within different departments that have access to information that can affect your role in the organization.

- Avoid associating titles with a person's level of authority or ability to make decisions. In some cases, the people with the most power or with access to valuable information can be lower on the organizational chart. For example, the President's scheduler not only has the ability to help you schedule a meeting with the President, but also can pass along information about upcoming issues that can affect your role within the organization.
- Identify and associate yourself with the organization's star employees. These are employees that are continually recognized and rewarded for their contributions to the organization. Introduce yourself to these employees and offer to assist them with their projects.

3. KNOW YOUR ROLE WITHIN YOUR ORGANIZATION

An important part of office politics is to know how your role affects other people and/or departments within the organization. The better you understand your role, the more power and influence you will have. This section describes how to determine what your role is within the organization.

- Determine why your position was created and what your responsibilities are.
- Look at the "big picture" of the projects you are assigned or the responsibilities you are given, and determine who will benefit from your work. Schedule meetings with those people/departments to discuss how you can best meet their needs.
- Evaluate who could potentially be threatened by your position. Schedule meetings with those people/departments to discuss steps that you can take to minimize their concerns.

4. MANAGING YOUR INFORMATION

Although having information, or access to it, is an important part of office politics, how you use that information will determine how successful you will be at managing office politics. Used correctly, the information you have can help you avoid conflicts. However, when used incorrectly, the information you have can create more conflicts than you care to deal with. This section will describe how to properly use the information you have to successfully manage office politics.

- Develop trust. If you are not sure if sharing the information you received is appropriate, consult the supplier of the information first. Using the information inappropriately can strain your relationship with your supplier and possibly cause you to develop a reputation as someone who is untrustworthy.
- Be a dependable and responsible resource of information. Always confirm your information before sharing it with others and only share information that adds value.
- Avoid passing on information that comes in the form of gossip. Gossip tends to contain very personal information, and in most cases the information has been skewed. Even if the information is true, passing on gossip can earn you a bad reputation very quickly.
- Never share personal information about others. If they want their personal information to become public, allow them to take on that responsibility themselves.

PERFORMANCE REVIEWS

A performance review is a tool utilized by organizations to provide employees feedback on their overall performance, as well as to provide management the means to evaluate employees for raises, promotions, and continued employment. This chapter will not only provide information on the different types of performance reviews, but also how to prepare for and react to them.

1. TYPES OF PERFORMANCE REVIEWS
The types and frequency of performance reviews vary from organization to organization. This section provides descriptions of the primary types of performance reviews.

Probationary Reviews
Organizations utilize probationary reviews to either evaluate new hires for possible full-time employment or to evaluate current employees that have performed poorly in the past. Probationary reviews not only provide the employee specific guidelines on how they will be evaluated for continued employment, but also provide the employer a means to protect themselves should an employee seek legal action against the organization for wrongful termination. Probationary review periods are typically between 30 and 180 days.

Semi-Annual Reviews

Although not as commonly used as an annual review, both types are used for the same purpose - to evaluate, reward, and in some cases, punish the performance of employees. Semi-annual reviews are often utilized as a method to provide new and current employees additional feedback on their performance, as well as to educate them on how they will be evaluated for continued employment, salary increases and promotions.

Self-Evaluation Reviews

Some large organizations may require that their employees conduct a self-evaluation prior to their performance reviews with their supervisor. Employees are usually instructed to complete and return these evaluations to their supervisors several days before their performance reviews. Because supervisors in large organizations must conduct several performance reviews in a short period of time, self-evaluations provide supervisors a brief synopsis of the employees' accomplishments, areas the employees perceive they need improvement, as well as the employees' goals for the upcoming year.

Annual Reviews

Annual reviews are the most common performance reviews utilized by organizations to evaluate their employees. The primary focus of an annual review is to evaluate and highlight an employee's performance and accomplishments over the past year, develop strategies to improve the employee's performance, discuss short and long term career goals, and determine if the employee is eligible for a salary increase or promotion. In some cases, an annual review is also an opportunity for an organization to inform an employee if he is not meeting the organization's expectations. If not, the individual is usually placed on probation and given a specific amount of time to improve his work.

2. UNDERSTANDING THE REVIEW PROCESS

One of the first tasks that you should complete as a new employee is to understand your organization's performance review process. By understanding what will be used as your measurements of success, who will be involved in the review process, when your performance review will take place, and how your performance review will be conducted, you will be better able to prepare and successfully complete your performance review.

To help you better understand the performance review process at your organization; consider some of the following helpful tips and suggestions.

- Request a copy of your job description as well as a blank performance review. Familiarize yourself with the duties you will be responsible for and how they correlate to the different categories and rating scales of the performance review.
- Schedule a meeting with your supervisor to discuss how you will be evaluated on your performance and determine what areas of your job are considered the most important.
- Visit with your fellow coworkers that have been through a performance review with your supervisor, and request their feedback on the overall process. Also request their opinions on areas of the performance review that they believed were important when they were being evaluated.

3. COLLECTING INFORMATION & GATHERING FEEDBACK
Collecting information and gathering feedback on your performance before your performance review occurs is essential to your success. Without this information you have little information to support the discussion of your accomplishments, skills and talents. In addition, you have little information to determine how you are performing in your position or what others think of your work. Provided below are several methods to use when collecting information and gathering feedback that will assist you in preparing for your performance review.

- Collect supporting information that demonstrates your success in your position, such as e-mails from your colleagues thanking you for your assistance with a project or certificates of completion for educational courses that you have taken.
- Request that your colleagues and clients inform your supervisor of exceptional work that you have completed. If appropriate, request a copy of the e-mail or letter that they provide to your supervisor for your records.
- Always ask for feedback from your colleagues, clients and supervisor on your performance. Avoid accepting general comments. Instead, ask for specific details on how you can perform better.

- Request that your supervisor give you more frequent informal performance reviews during your first few months in a new position to ensure that you are meeting his expectations.
- Review job descriptions of positions that you want to be promoted to in the future and begin developing the skills that will assist you in meeting the requirements for those positions. For example, attend educational seminars or attend classes at a local college or university.

4. PREPARING FOR YOUR PERFORMANCE REVIEW

In most organizations, a supervisor is responsible for the management of several employees. Part of that responsibility includes conducting performance reviews of the employees he oversees. As you can imagine, keeping track of the accomplishments that each employee contributes to the organization can be overwhelming. Therefore, it is in your best interest to help your supervisor recall your accomplishments before your performance review takes place. In addition, it is important that you prepare yourself for any potential areas of concern that may be addressed during your performance review. This section describes several tools that you can provide to your supervisor before your performance review takes place to assist him in recalling your accomplishments, to inform him of your goals, and to prepare you for any areas of concern during your performance review.

- Develop a summary report of your accomplishments to provide to your supervisor at least one week before your performance review takes place. Organize the summary in a similar fashion as you would a resume. For example, highlight important projects you completed or participated in and provide bullet points emphasizing the skills that you utilized as well as the results that the project provided to the organization. In addition, add sections to your summary report that describe skills that you are developing as well as your career goals. Try to limit your summary report to one page to ensure that your supervisor will read the entire document. (A sample summary report is provided on the next page.)
- Organize documents or other information that supports your summary report, such as letters of recommendation from colleagues and clients or certificates of completion from seminars or educational courses that you attended. Bring these documents and other relevant information to your performance review to present to your supervisor.

Performance Review Summary Report
For "Bill Briefcase" *(1/1/XX – 12/31/XX)*

PROJECT ACCOMPLISHMENTS

Development of the Advertising Program for *XYZ Magazine*

- Conducted numerous marketing surveys among our readers to develop a complete demographic analysis that enabled us to attract interest among advertisers in our readers.
- Created our media kit (attached) with the assistance of our Graphics & Communications Department.
- Exceeded first-year advertising revenue goals by 173% while only utilizing 64% of the budget.

Increasing New and Renewal Subscriptions of *XYZ Magazine*

- Organized regional focus groups with the assistance of our Marketing Department to identify key issues to be addressed in *XYZ Magazine* that are important to our readers.
- Organized informational luncheon meetings where subscription staff were provided short educational sessions to learn how to negotiate and close sales, and develop personal sales goals.
- Worked with Betsy Backpack, Director of New Sales, in organizing an appropriate incentive program for her staff.

Creation of XYZ, Inc.'s Management Retreat

- After identifying the need for better communication among departments, I met with department heads to create an outline for how our organization can communicate more effectively. Management then participated in a two-day retreat that I organized to review the outline for a more effective communication program. The retreat was successful in developing our current communication program. In addition, management has requested the need for additional retreats to discuss other organizational issues.

EDUCATION & TRAINING

- Completion of my MBA from State University. Areas of focus include Advertising, Marketing and Entrepreneurship.
- Attended the Time Management and Effective Marketing Seminars conducted by the Association of Young Professionals.
- Current Member and Chair of the New Member Committee for the Association of Advertising Professionals.

GOALS

With my direct involvement in the development and overall success of *XYZ Magazine's* advertising program, the successful completion of my MBA, and my dedication to the overall success of XYZ, Inc., I believe that I am an excellent candidate for the new Director of Advertising position.

- Review your job description and a blank copy of your organization's performance review (or previous performance reviews that you have received) and locate possible areas of concern that your supervisor may raise with you during your performance review. Develop a response for each of these areas of concern and provide supporting documentation to demonstrate the steps that you are taking, or have taken, to correct the concern. For example, if you suspect your supervisor is concerned about your understanding of the organization's database software, you can inform him that you were having difficulty understanding how to input and use the information in the database. However, you have since attended several courses offered by the database manufacturer (provide your supervisor certificates of completion). In addition, explain that you are now using the skills that you have learned to teach new employees how to use the database effectively.

5. DURING THE PERFORMANCE REVIEW

In a way, a performance review is similar to a job interview. Therefore, it is extremely important that while your performance review is being conducted, you not only put your best foot forward, but you also listen and learn from the process. The following bullet points provide several tips and suggestions on what to do during your performance review.

- Present yourself in a professional manner. For example, dress appropriately and communicate effectively.
- Avoid becoming defensive or arguing with your supervisor. Remember, part of the performance review process will include some professional criticism. Therefore, when professional criticism is presented, be sure to listen to the criticism, ask questions to clarify why your supervisor believes you need improvement, and learn what you can do to show your supervisor that you have improved.
- Take notes during your performance review. Although your supervisor may provide you a copy of your review, it will most likely be provided to you in a summary format. Therefore, keep track of key topics or issues that your supervisor spends a significant amount of time discussing, and learn what issues are most important to him.
- Turn negatives into positives. Focusing on negative issues, or areas of improvement, for a significant amount of time during a performance review is easy to do, but often not beneficial to your overall performance

review. Although it is important to understand how to improve yourself, you want to take every opportunity that you can to bring up positive issues. For example, if your supervisor is discussing how he believes you need to improve your computer skills, discuss that issue with him, but in doing so, be sure to mention how you recently enrolled in a computer course at the local community college to improve your skills.

- Self-promote yourself. Remember, this is an opportunity when your supervisor is expecting you to highlight your accomplishments. Therefore, be sure to take full advantage of this opportunity. You may find it helpful to review the "Self-Promotion" chapter for more information.

- Always show your appreciation and thank your supervisor when he acknowledges your accomplishments or offers suggestions on how to improve yourself. By doing so, you are informing your supervisor that you value his feedback.

6. AFTER THE PERFORMANCE REVIEW

Regardless of whether you receive a poor, average or great performance review, use the information from the review process to prepare for your next performance review. To assist you in this process, be sure to complete the following tasks.

- Review any documents that your supervisor provides you during or after the performance review, as well as the notes you took during the performance review, and highlight the areas that you will need to improve upon.

- Develop a strategic plan on how you will improve yourself in those areas. For example, if one of your goals is to communicate more effectively with your supervisor, you might suggest providing your supervisor weekly reports, scheduling informal feedback sessions every quarter, or even attending an effective communication seminar.

- Share your strategic plan with your supervisor to gather her feedback, comments and suggestions. In addition, request that a copy of your strategic plan be added to your permanent file and used as a reference during your next performance review.

- Maintain a record of the steps that you took to complete your strategic plan. Be sure to provide your supervisor updates on your progress.

7. RECEIVING A POOR PERFORMANCE REVIEW

Receiving a poor performance review is not an enjoyable experience and hopefully not an experience that you will have to encounter. If you do receive a poor performance review, seriously consider implementing the steps provided in the previous sections. However, if you believe that your poor performance review does not accurately reflect your work and contributions, then consider the following tips and suggestions.

- Review your performance review and develop a written rebuttal providing examples of your skills and accomplishments that contradict what was described in your performance review.
- Schedule a follow-up meeting with your supervisor to discuss your performance review. Prior to the meeting, provide your supervisor a copy of your rebuttal to allow him time to review and research the issues that you wish to discuss.
- During your meeting, review your rebuttal with your supervisor. If for some reason you and your supervisor can not come to an agreement on your performance review and/or you believe that there is a personality conflict between you and your supervisor, request that your rebuttal be added to your personnel file and consider contacting your Human Resource Department or a representative from upper management about the situation and request their assistance in resolving the matter.
- Regardless of the situation, avoid becoming angry or defensive as this will only make the situation worse.

PROFESSIONAL ATTIRE

When deciding what attire to wear to work, your decision needs to be based on more than what you think makes you look good. Factors to consider include your line of work, the environment you are working in, and your audience. This chapter will focus on each of these factors, as well as provide you helpful tips and suggestions for developing a professional wardrobe on a limited budget.

1. YOUR LINE OF WORK

The line of work you choose often will determine the type of attire you will wear to work. Outlined below are three general types of careers, the common attire for each, as well as the message that the attire you choose to wear should send to others.

Traditional Careers

Positions:	Legal, Financial and Government
How to Dress:	Conservative business attire
Message:	Wear clothing that sends a message that you have authority and are competent.

People Oriented Careers

Positions:	Education, Sales, Medical and Social
How to Dress:	Traditional business attire
Message:	Wear clothing that sends a message that you are trustworthy, approachable and knowledgeable.

Creative/Artistic Careers

Positions:	Advertising, Fashion, and Entertainment
How to Dress:	Contemporary business attire
Message:	Wear clothing that sends a message that you are creative and unique.

2. YOUR OFFICE ENVIRONMENT

Although general guidelines regarding appropriate attire for an industry or specific career, such as the ones provided in the previous section, can be helpful, they are certainly not full proof. For example, within the legal industry, there are a variety of careers to choose from. Thus, what may be appropriate attire for an attorney practicing general law in a small beach community in Florida may not necessarily be appropriate for a tax attorney working for a large accounting firm in New York City. Therefore, it is important to evaluate your office environment when determining what is appropriate attire. Provided below are a few suggestions to keep in mind when determining what is appropriate attire for your office environment.

- Most employers provide their employees some form of a dress code. If your employer does not, chances are that there is an unspoken policy. Consult your supervisor about what they believe is appropriate attire for your position.
- Evaluate the types of clothing your colleagues' wear over a period of time. For example, do they tend to dress up on certain days of the week and dress down on other days?
- Determine the variety of clothing your colleagues' wear. Do they diversify certain pieces of clothing, such as wearing standard color suits and varying the shirt and tie or blouse, or do they wear a completely different outfit every day?
- Estimate how much money your colleagues spend on their clothing. Do they wear high quality or standard quality clothing? Also, do your colleagues wear the latest fashions or fashion neutral clothing?

3. YOUR AUDIENCE

The people whom you interact with in your position play an important role in determining what is appropriate attire for you to wear. For example, you might think a salesperson representing $150,000 to $500,000 equipment would wear a suit when conducting a sales call. However, a suit may not be appropriate attire for a salesperson whose client happens to be a farmer looking to purchase a $300,000 harvester.   By understanding your audience, you can better judge what attire will be appropriate for you to wear. Therefore, consult your supervisor to determine whom you will be interacting with in your position. For example, will your interactions be limited to your colleagues in the office, will clients and potential customers frequently visit your workplace, or are you required to make on-site visits to clients and potential customers?

When evaluating what attire best fits your audience, keep in mind not only what attire allows you to relate to them, but also what image they perceive someone in your position should look like.   Therefore, if your audience primarily includes farmers, and their attire includes jeans, work boots and baseball caps, they may perceive a salesperson representing a manufacturer of high-priced harvesters wearing the exact same attire as them to be unprofessional and incapable of providing the professional support they expect after the sale. A better choice of attire in this situation may be a button down shirt, pressed slacks and leather casual shoes.

Although this example is a bit extreme, it does reinforce the importance of understanding your audience, how best to relate to them and what image they perceive someone in your position should look like.

4. WHAT TO PURCHASE & WHEN
When starting a new job, not only is it important to determine what is appropriate attire for your new position, but also when is an appropriate time for you to purchase new attire. This section provides several helpful tips to consider when determining what type of attire to purchase, what type of attire you should avoid purchasing, as well as when you should purchase your attire.

Attire You Need
Regardless of the type of job or the position you accept, there is certain professional and casual attire you should have in your wardrobe. This section provides examples of professional and casual attire for men and women.

Men

Professional
Dark colored suit
Long sleeve dress shirt
Traditional colored tie
Black or dark colored dress shoes

Casual
Jacket is optional
Button down shirt
Pressed slacks
Leather casual shoes

Women

Professional
Dark colored skirt suit
Traditional blouse
Dark colored, mid-heel dress shoes
Dark hose

Casual
Jacket is optional
Blouse, sweater or twin set
Skirt or pressed slacks
Low heeled shoes

Attire You Should Avoid

There is certain attire that does not belong in the work place. A common rule of thumb is that if you are unsure if a piece of clothing is appropriate, do not wear it to work. Provided below are just a few examples of what you should avoid wearing at work.

- Jeans. However, if your company occasionally allows employees to wear jeans, wear jeans that are clean and not faded or frayed.
- Athletic attire and relaxed accessories, such as T-shirts, baseball caps or warm-ups.
- Revealing clothing, such as low-cut or tight tops, short skirts or skirts with high slits.
- Relaxed or party shoes, such as sneakers, sandals, or extremely high heels.

When To Purchase Attire For Work

Determining what is appropriate attire for your new job takes some time to evaluate. In addition, having the money to purchase new attire takes time to accumulate. Be sure to consider the following suggestions when you have determined the appropriate attire you will need for your new job.

- Before beginning a new job, you often do not have the luxury of evaluating the work environment or your audience. However, you can determine if professional or casual attire is acceptable. Therefore, for at least the first week or two, utilize the attire described in the "Attire You Need" section of this chapter.

- Until you have the financial resources available to purchase a complete wardrobe of work clothes without going into debt, purchase clothing that is both versatile and diverse.
- If money is tight, but you need high-quality business attire, consider purchasing clothing from a professional consignment shop. These shops are readily found in most cities and usually carry high-quality clothing that are in excellent condition and are reasonably priced.
- In order to utilize your clothing year-round, consider purchasing clothing made of multi-purpose fabrics and neutral colors.
- Accessorize. Adding accessories is an inexpensive method of making your wardrobe appear larger than it is. Accessories can include blouses, ties, shoes, belts, handbags and designer jewelry.
- Avoid purchasing a large amount of clothing at once. Instead, purchase your work attire over an extended period of time. This allows you additional time to evaluate your work environment and audience, as well as time to properly budget your clothing purchases. In addition, it allows you to keep your wardrobe up-to-date with the current fashions.

RAISES & PROMOTIONS

Instinctively, one of the first items that every employee thinks about after starting a new job is what do they need to do to receive a raise or promotion. The interesting part about this situation is that most employees already know what they need to do – work hard, exceed expectations, show initiative, etc. However, what they fail to realize is that raises and promotions are rarely just "handed out," employees must ask for them. This section not only provides you the tools you need to ask for a raise or promotion, but also how to do so effectively and persuasively.

1. UNDERSTANDING THE PROCESS

To successfully receive a raise or promotion, you must first learn your organization's procedures for receiving a raise or promotion. Although you may decide that following your organization's procedures does not fit your specific needs, understanding the process may provide you valuable information on the specific steps you must follow in order to be successful in your request. The following tips and suggestions describe how to gather this information.

- Review your organization's employee handbook. Often organizations will include a section describing employee evaluations, such as how and when they are conducted.
- Contact your Human Resource Department and request information on the procedures for requesting a raise or promotion. For example, when are raises and promotions awarded, who determines which employees

receive a raise or promotion, and does the organization have an
established level for the size of a raise or promotion an employee can
receive?

- Visit with your colleagues and ask them about the organization's recent
history for awarding employees raises and promotions, as well as their
recommendations for what you need to do in order to receive a raise or
promotion.

2. WHEN TO REQUEST A RAISE/PROMOTION

Knowing when to request a raise or promotion is essential to your success in
obtaining a raise or promotion. As mentioned in the previous section, your
organization may have an established timeframe for when raises and
promotions are considered, such as during your annual review. However,
this established time might not necessarily meet your needs. Therefore, if
you are considering requesting a raise or promotion outside of your
organization's established timeframe, be sure to consider these examples of
situations when it may be appropriate to request a raise or promotion.

- Your organization is experiencing new successes as a direct result of
your contributions.
- Your organization is currently reviewing or developing budgets for the
upcoming quarter or year.
- Your organization is struggling and your presence is essential to its
future success.
- You have been provided an offer for employment with another
organization for a significant increase in salary or benefits.
- Your supervisor has expressed to you his approval of your contributions
to the organization.
- You are aware of discrepancies in your compensation in comparison to
your colleagues or the compensation of comparable positions with
competing organizations.

3. TYPES OF RAISES & PROMOTIONS

Often when employees think of raises and promotions, they think of some
form of financial compensation. Although an increase in salary is great,
there are a number of other options to consider when requesting a raise or
promotion. This section describes the three primary types of raises and
promotions.

- **Increase in Financial Compensation**
  An increase in financial compensation can be in the form of an increase in your salary, commission rate or as a bonus.
- **Increase in Title**
  An increase in title is often overlooked as an option for a raise or promotion. However, a title can provide access to more power, responsibilities, opportunities and benefits. These benefits all equate to better opportunities to increase your financial compensation at a later date. In addition, a better title can be helpful when pursuing a career with a new organization.
- **Increase in Benefits**
  An increase in benefits is often the easiest type of raise and promotion to receive. This can include additional vacation time or a better office space. Although the financial expense associated with awarding these types of raises and promotions is minor as compared to some of the other options, organizations will often utilize these options when they do not have the ability to award other forms of raises or promotions.

4. PREPARING TO REQUEST A RAISE/PROMOTION

A large part of receiving a raise or promotion is asking for it. However, before you ask for a raise or promotion, there are several steps you should consider taking in order for your request to have the best chance for success. This section describes those steps.

Gather Evidence Of Your Accomplishments/Contributions

Gathering evidence to prove your accomplishments and contributions is identical to collecting information for a performance review. Therefore, to learn more about gathering evidence of your accomplishments and contributions, review the "Performance Reviews" chapter.

Determine Your Worth

Almost every employee believes their efforts at work are worth more than they receive in compensation. Providing evidence that justifies receiving adequate compensation can be difficult. However, having this evidence to provide to your supervisor is invaluable to your success in obtaining a raise or promotion. The following bullet points provide methods that you can use in determining your worth.

- Contact the trade association that represents your profession. As a value to their membership, some trade associations will conduct compensation and benefits surveys and provide these results to their members. In some cases, this information is broken-up by job title, region, years of experience, etc.
- Contact recruitment firms that assist people in your profession to locate new jobs. These firms often have a wide range of supporting documents regarding average compensation and benefit packages to assist recruits determine the "market rate" for new and experienced employees.
- Visit employment-related list-serves, bulletin boards, or chat rooms on the Internet for current compensation information.
- Request assistance from your mentor. If your mentor is unaware of current compensation programs for employees with your experience, he may be able to contact his colleagues for the information.
- Network with professionals outside of your organization to determine what they believe is fair compensation for your experience and talents.
- Determine what other employees in your organization are earning. Because salary and compensation are very personal information, coworkers are often hesitant about offering this information. However, employees that have recently left the organization may be more open to sharing information about their previous compensation program.
- Review the employment classified listings in your local and regional newspapers or on the Internet. Many organizations will provide general compensation information in their listings.

Develop A Realistic Raise/Promotion Request
After gathering evidence of your accomplishments and contributions, as well as conducting research to determine your worth, you need to develop a request for a realistic raise or promotion that you believe you deserve. Keep in mind that the raise or promotion that you request from your supervisor will be considered the starting point for negotiating what you receive. Also remember that you never know what is available unless you ask for it!

Create A "Raise/Promotion Request Memorandum"
Before requesting a salary or promotion from your supervisor, prepare a "Raise/Promotion Request Memorandum". This is recommended for several reasons. First, it will provide your supervisor a quick review of what you are requesting, as well as provide your supervisor supporting information justifying your request. Second, it provides you a quick

reference guide to refer to as you discuss your proposal for a raise or promotion with your supervisor. Finally, because your supervisor may need to receive approval from someone in upper management before awarding you a raise or promotion, your "Raise/Promotion Request Memorandum" sheet will provide your supervisor the information he will need to assist him with this process. A sample memorandum is provided on the next page.

In addition to the "Raise/Promotion Request Memorandum," your request for a raise or promotion should include the following information.

- Your "Raise/Promotion Summary Report". This sheet highlights your accomplishments, skills, education, training, and goals. See the sample "Raise/Promotion Summary Report" on page 107.
- Documents or information that support your "Raise/Promotion Request Memorandum", such as letters of recommendation from colleagues and clients or certificates of completion from seminars or educational courses that you completed. Also, include any information that you have gathered regarding appropriate compensation for your position.

Develop A "Sales Pitch"

You are probably familiar with the term "sales pitch." This is a short statement that a salesperson will use to quickly develop interest among potential customers in the product or service he is selling. If the sales pitch is done well, the customer is interested in learning more about what the salesperson has to offer. However, if the sales pitch is weak, the potential customer becomes uninterested and begins focusing on reasons not to purchase the product or service. Requesting a raise or promotion is very similar to selling a product or service. Therefore, similar to the salesperson example, you must develop your own sales pitch that will win the interest of your supervisor. This section provides you some tips and suggestions to keep in mind as you develop your sales pitch. In addition, a sample sales pitch has been provided for you on page 108.

- Be quick. Your sales pitch should only take you one to two minutes to present to your supervisor.
- Be concise. Avoid discussing all the details of your request. Simply provide enough information that will develop interest in what you are requesting.

Sample "Raise/Promotion Request Memorandum"

To: Ms. Sally Supervisor

From: Bill Briefcase

Date: January 14

Re: Request For Promotion To Director of Advertising

I have worked for XYZ, Inc. for 2 years as Assistant Director of Marketing and Membership. Over the past 9 months, the focus of my position has been developing programs to increase advertising revenues for our periodicals. During this time, I have worked hard to exceed our advertising sales goals. In fact, as a direct result of my efforts, we have exceeded our advertising sales goals by 117%, providing XYZ, Inc. an additional $3.4 million in revenue.

As you are aware, the Board of Directors of XYZ, Inc. has recently approved the implementation of a new Advertising Department, as a result of a financial viability report that I developed. In that report, I described the growing demands on the resources of the Marketing and Membership Department that have resulted in the reduced growth of our membership. In addition, I described how the addition of an Advertising Department would allow the Marketing and Membership Department to reallocate their resources to grow membership by 12% next year.

The new Advertising Department will oversee all advertising sales, promotions and programs. According to my projections, this new department will add an additional $4.6 million of revenue in the first year alone.

I understand XYZ, Inc. is currently searching for qualified candidates to serve as Director of Advertising. I believe my success in developing our current advertising program, as well as my recent MBA from State University, provides me the skills necessary to oversee our Advertising Department. Therefore, I request that I be promoted as XYZ, Inc.'s new Director of Advertising.

ATTACHMENTS:
- "Raise/Promotion Summary Report"
- Letter of Recommendation from Mr. Marketing - Director of Marketing, XYZ, Inc.

Raise/Promotion Summary Report
For "Bill Briefcase" *(1/1/XX – 12/31/XX)*

PROJECT ACCOMPLISHMENTS

Development of the Advertising Program for *XYZ Magazine*

- Conducted numerous marketing surveys among our readers to develop a complete demographic analysis that enabled us to attract interest among advertisers in our readers.
- Created our media kit (attached) with the assistance of our Graphics & Communications Department.
- Exceeded first-year advertising revenue goals by 173% while only utilizing 64% of the budget.

Increasing New and Renewal Subscriptions of *XYZ Magazine*

- Organized regional focus groups with the assistance of our Marketing Department to identify key issues to be addressed in *XYZ Magazine* that are important to our readers.
- Organized informational luncheon meetings where subscription staff were provided short educational sessions to learn how to negotiate and close sales, and develop personal sales goals.
- Worked with Betsy Backpack, Director of New Sales, in organizing an appropriate incentive program for her staff.

Creation of XYZ, Inc.'s Management Retreat

- After identifying the need for better communication among departments, I met with department heads to create an outline for how our organization can communicate more effectively. Management then participated in a two-day retreat that I organized to review the outline for a more effective communication program. The retreat was successful in developing our current communication program. In addition, management has requested the need for additional retreats to discuss other organizational issues.

EDUCATION & TRAINING

- Completion of my MBA from State University. Areas of focus include Advertising, Marketing and Entrepreneurship.
- Attended the Time Management and Effective Marketing Seminars conducted by the Association of Young Professionals.
- Current Member and Chair of the New Member Committee for the Association of Advertising Professionals.

GOALS

With my direct involvement in the development and overall success of *XYZ Magazine's* advertising program, the successful completion of my MBA, and my dedication to the overall success of XYZ, Inc., I believe that I am an excellent candidate for the new Director of Advertising position.

Sample "Sales Pitch"

"Mr. Supervisor, as you are aware, I have worked for XYZ, Inc. for two years. In that time, as you have recognized on many occasions, I have worked hard to ensure that I not only met all of my sales goals, but also exceeded them. In fact, last year I exceeded my sales goal by 117%, providing XYZ, Inc. an additional $3.4 million in revenue. I have enjoyed the challenges this position has provided me, and I am ready to accept new challenges. Therefore, I am requesting that I be promoted to Director of Advertising."

Develop An Agenda

Like a business meeting, a raise or promotion request requires an agenda to ensure control over how and when information will be presented. However, unlike a business meeting where everyone involved receives a copy of the agenda, the agenda for your raise or promotion request is developed for your use only. When developing your agenda, keep in mind the following items.

- Show your value to the organization. Summarize your past accomplishments, development of skills, and education. Be sure to emphasize important points, such as exceeding goals, increasing profits, reducing costs, etc.
- Provide a comparison of your current compensation program to the compensation programs of employees with similar experience and background at comparable organizations. If you do not have this type of information, provide any information from your research that offers validity to your request for a raise or promotion.
- Offer your request for a raise or promotion. This is the time when you should provide your supervisor a copy of your "Raise / Promotion Request Memorandum."
- Stop, watch and listen. Although this is difficult for most people to do, allow your supervisor to absorb the information you have just provided to him. Watch your supervisor's body language to determine his approval or disapproval of your request, and then listen to what your supervisor has to say when he responds to your request.
- Answer questions. There will no doubt be questions regarding the information that you have presented. Therefore, review your agenda and the information you will be presenting, and locate possible questions that your supervisor may bring up during your meeting. In addition, be sure to develop answers for these possible questions.

Practice Makes Perfect

When requesting a raise or promotion, avoid making mistakes, as mistakes will have a negative effect on your request. Therefore, be sure to practice your request. The more practice, the better. Recruit a friend, relative or spouse to act as your supervisor as you present your sales pitch and agenda. Request that they ask you questions, critique your delivery, and offer suggestions on how to make your presentation better. Remember, requesting a raise or promotion is very important. Therefore, dedicate enough time for practicing to ensure your presentation is as perfect as possible.

5. REQUESTING A RAISE/PROMOTION

When the time has come to meet with your supervisor and request a raise or promotion, be sure to keep the following tips and suggestions in mind.

- Be prepared. In addition to developing an agenda and having the appropriate documents available to support your request, be sure to have two copies of your "Raise/Promotion Request Memorandum" available. One sheet is for you to refer to during your presentation and the other sheet is to be provided to your supervisor for him to review.
- Avoid becoming nervous, anxious or scared. Relax and focus on your accomplishments and the contributions that you have made to the organization.
- Maintain a positive attitude. Becoming negative or angry will only cause your supervisor to feel the same way or may even cause him to become defensive.
- Never use threats or demands. No one enjoys being told what to do or being put into a situation where they must do something. Instead, use the information that you have gathered to educate and persuade your supervisor into granting your request for a raise or promotion.
- Do not use desperation as a reason for a raise or promotion, such as financial hardship or medical problems.
- Schedule a follow-up meeting. If your supervisor is not prepared to grant, counter-offer, or decline your request for a raise or promotion, schedule a follow-up meeting. Avoid agreeing to a non-committal date for a follow-up meeting, such as "come by some time next week" or "let me get back to you." Instead, set a specific date and time.

- Thank your supervisor for his time and consideration. Remember, you have just asked your supervisor to complete a very important task for you. Therefore, be sure to show your appreciation.

6. THE RESPONSE

After meeting with your supervisor to request a raise or promotion, you will receive one of two responses, yes or no. However, the response you receive can have several meanings. Therefore, before reacting to your supervisor's decision, be sure to consider the following items.

The Yes Response

If you performed well, and you provided convincing evidence in requesting a raise or promotion, chances are you will receive some type of raise or promotion. Consider the following items when evaluating and accepting your raise or promotion.

- Be prepared to negotiate. In most situations, you will receive a counter-offer to your request. If so, determine why you are not being offered what you had originally requested, develop a convincing response, and suggest a counter-offer. For example, you request a $5,000 salary increase. Your supervisor states that because of budget cuts she is only able to offer you a $1,000 salary increase. You can respond by stating that you understand that there have been budget cuts; however, even with recent departmental budget cuts you have been able to continue your department's growth, and in fact have increased profits by 48% or $2.7 million. Therefore, it is difficult for you to understand how increasing profits by $2.7 million does not warrant more of a salary increase than $1,000, and you hope that she will seriously reconsider her decision.
- Should you not receive the entire raise or promotion you requested, ask your supervisor to provide you with goals that you need to accomplish in order to receive the raise and promotion you desire. Make a list of these goals and develop a strategic plan to accomplish them. Be sure to keep your supervisor aware of your progress in obtaining these goals.
- Regardless of the size of your raise or promotion, thank your supervisor for acknowledging your hard work and express your appreciation by writing your supervisor a thank you note.

- Honor your supervisor's requests. For example, if you requested and were awarded a raise or promotion at a time that the organization traditionally does not award raises and promotions, your supervisor might request that you not inform your coworkers of your raise or promotion in order to limit additional requests from other employees.
- Be conscious of your coworkers. After being awarded a raise or promotion, do not gloat about it to your coworkers. This can cause tension and frustration among your coworkers, which can hinder further progress in your position.

The No Response
Unfortunately, you will not always be awarded a raise or promotion with each request you submit. Not receiving a raise or promotion does not necessarily mean that your efforts in doing so were not conducted properly or were not valid. There may be extenuating circumstances that you are not aware of that have inhibited your supervisor from granting any raises or promotions. Therefore, before accepting no as an answer, consider the following items.

- Avoid becoming frustrated, defensive or angry. Although being denied something you believe you deserve is difficult to accept, remember that your actions have consequences. Therefore, maintain your composure and learn as much as you can from the experience.
- Determine the reason you were not awarded the raise or promotion. For example, does your work not meet the criteria for a raise or promotion, or is the organization unable to grant raises and promotions due to financial constraints? Whatever the reason, gather specific information that can assist you in obtaining a raise or promotion at a later date.
- Consider negotiating for a smaller raise or promotion. Your initial request may have been too specific or too demanding. Therefore, consider offering other options for your supervisor to consider, such as requesting a smaller increase in your salary or performance-related compensation, such as receiving a bonus for exceeding goals.
- Ask your supervisor to provide you goals that you need to accomplish in order to receive the raise or promotion you desire. Make a list of these goals and develop a strategic plan to accomplish them. Be sure to keep your supervisor aware of your progress in obtaining these goals.

- Request a re-evaluation of your salary or promotion request before your next annual or semi-annual review, such as in three months. Doing so will allow you the possible opportunity to be awarded your raise or promotion much earlier than if you wait.
- Thank your supervisor for his time, consideration and feedback.

7. THE FREQUENCY OF YOUR REQUESTS

This chapter has provided you valuable information about how and when to request a raise or promotion. Although it is up to you to determine when it is appropriate to request a raise or promotion, be sure to keep in mind that requesting a raise or promotion too frequently can have negative consequences. For example, requesting a raise or promotion too frequently will cause your requests to have little or no impact as your boss may perceive your frequent requests as a sign that you will never be satisfied, no matter what he offers you. Therefore, before requesting a raise or promotion, be sure to choose an opportunity to present your request that you believe will provide you the best chance of obtaining a potential raise or promotion.

SELF-PROMOTION

Although you may think that hard work and dedication are all that it takes to be recognized as a good employee, this is not always the case. More often than not, it is the effective self-promoters that are usually the employees that receive the most recognition for their efforts. Self-promotion is the skill of informing others of your talents, contributions and successes in an inconspicuous and non-threatening manner. Performing self-promotion successfully will often result in a raise, promotion or other beneficial perks. However, performing self-promotion poorly can be perceived as arrogance and/or result in developing a reputation as a "brown-noser." This chapter will provide you several characteristics of effective self-promoters as well as suggestions on how to effectively self-promote yourself.

1. CHARACTERISTICS OF EFFECTIVE SELF-PROMOTERS

To become an effective self-promoter, you need to develop certain characteristics that enable you to develop a reputation as someone who deserves recognition. Listed below are several characteristics you should develop in order to become a successful self-promoter.

- **Enthusiasm**
  Employees that are enthusiastic are chosen to become leaders and to spread their enthusiasm within the organization.
- **Initiative**
  Employees that are willing to put forth the extra effort and get involved in projects without being asked are recognized as "go-getters."

- **Creativity**
  Employees that offer new ideas are often put into positions that allow them the opportunity to follow through with their ideas.
- **Opportunist**
  Employees that participate in opportunities that allow them to be put in the forefront are more likely to be recognized for promotions and raises.
- **Confidence**
  Employees that express and demonstrate confidence in their skills and abilities are often provided opportunities that allow them to "show off" their talents.
- **Trustworthy**
  Employees that can be trusted are employees that will be given more responsibilities. The more responsibilities you have, the more valuable you become to the organization.

2. HOW TO SELF-PROMOTE YOURSELF

Once you have developed the characteristics of an effective self-promoter, you will find that you will have numerous opportunities to self-promote yourself. When these opportunities develop, it is important that you take advantage of them. Provided below are some tips, suggestions and examples on how to accomplish this.

- Avoid too much self-promotion. Instead, focus your efforts on major accomplishments, such as securing a new client, or situations that will provide you the most recognition, such as discussing the status of a big project you are working on during a staff or board meeting.
- Use office communications to self-promote yourself. For example, when having to work late, send your supervisor an e-mail regarding the status of your project. Since your e-mail records the date and time it was sent, you boss will see that you were working late. In addition, be sure to forward your supervisor any e-mails from your colleagues and clients that acknowledge your successful performance on a project.
- Have others assist you in your self-promotion. For example, encourage clients to contact your supervisors about the level of service you have provided them.
- Participate in highly visible projects, such as becoming a member of the team assigned the task of developing a new marketing program to increase company profits.

- Inform your supervisors of the accomplishments of your colleagues. Doing so provides several benefits, such as gaining the respect of your teammates, as well as being recognized by your supervisors as a leader that is willing to put your teammates in the forefront.
- Offer to assist your colleagues with their projects or request additional responsibilities. This will provide you more exposure within your organization, as well as make you more valuable to the organization.
- Volunteer for projects that allow you the opportunity to present your work to upper management. In addition, build relationships with upper management in other departments by offering your assistance on projects that they are working on.
- Utilize meetings and presentations to suggest ideas, raise pertinent questions, and demonstrate your knowledge.
- Learn to accept praise and avoid downplaying your accomplishments. For instance, when someone praises you, say "Thank You" instead of, "Oh, it was nothing."
- Become an active participant in your industries' trade association and share your work and accomplishments with your supervisors. For example, become an active member of the trade association's grassroots lobbying effort and offer to provide updates on your efforts at your staff meeting or through an inter-office memo or e-mail.

TEAMWORK

In today's business environment, more and more organizations are moving away from traditional management methods and implementing the use of teams as a way to increase efficiency and productivity. This change has created a demand for employees that not only understand the value of a team, but also know what skills are needed to be an effective team player. To ensure that you are prepared to work in a team environment, this chapter highlights the information you will need to know in order to be a successful team player.

1. WHAT IS TEAMWORK?

The primary difference between traditional methods of management and allowing teams to manage projects (teamwork) is that upper management is empowering the team, instead of a manager, to make key decisions. Following is a comparison of these two management methods.

The Traditional Management Method

Under the traditional management method, upper management will assign a project to a manager to complete. The manager reviews the project, as well as the skills of his staff. He then breaks up the project into smaller projects and assigns each of these smaller projects, along with specific instructions on how to complete them, to various individuals within his department. Once all of the smaller projects are completed, the leader then collects the information and puts it together in a format that he believes will best meet the needs of upper management.

The Teamwork Management Method

Under the teamwork management method, upper management will assign a project to a team leader. The team leader reviews the project, as well as the skills and characteristics of various individuals within the organization. He then puts together a group of individuals that he believes has the skills and characteristics that can successfully work together to complete the project. Other than being provided some occasional guidance from the team leader, the team is given full responsibility to determine how to best utilize each other's skills and talents to accomplish the project.

2. CHARACTERISTICS OF AN EFFECTIVE TEAM

Unfortunately, developing an effective team takes more than combining a group of random people together and providing them a project to accomplish. Not only does it take time and research to pick the correct people to complete the task, but the team must also be provided the information and resources necessary to complete the project successfully. Listed below are a few of the items to consider when choosing a team.

- The team must be capable of taking responsibility and accepting credit for its actions as a group and not individually.
- The team must consist of individuals that are committed to a common purpose and goal.
- The team must be provided clear expectations for its performance and outcomes.
- The team must be provided adequate resources to accomplish its agenda and goals.
- Members of the team must avoid the use of words or actions that inhibit other members from proposing new ideas, such as saying "no way," or rolling their eyes when another team member proposes a new idea.
- Members of the team must have complementary skills and be able to communicate effectively with each other.
- Members of the team must put the team's goals ahead of their own self-interests.
- Members of the team must be trustworthy.
- Members of the team must avoid conflicts when challenges occur, and instead offer suggestions on how the team can overcome challenges.
- Members of the team must know how to listen effectively and be open to new ideas or concepts.

- Members of the team must learn to appreciate the diversity of knowledge that the other team members have to offer.
- Members of the team must be creative and unafraid to share their opinions, ideas and suggestions.

3. TEAM LEADERSHIP

An important part of an effective team is having an effective team leader. Unlike other management styles where the manager tends to be directly involved in all aspects of the project, a team leader has a very limited role in what a team does. The duties of a team leader usually involve the following items.

- Reviews the skills and characteristics of the organization's employees and chooses a team to accomplish the project.
- Acts as a liaison between upper management and the team.
- Informs the team of the project to be accomplished, the time frame in which the project is to be completed, as well as any other limitations that upper management may have.
- Provides guidance and support as needed to ensure that the team stays on track.
- Manages the teams' members to minimize conflicts and to ensure that compatibility exists.

4. WHY TEAMS FAIL

Although teams tend to be an effective method for accomplishing various tasks, not all teams are successful. In most cases, teams fail because they lack the proper leadership. However, there are other factors that can cause a team to fail that are out of the team leader's control. The following bullet points highlight several reasons why teams fail, as well as what can be done to help teams from failing.

- The team experiences "groupthink." Groupthink occurs when one or more individuals in a group propose an idea or concept that the rest of the group decides is the best without considering other alternatives or options. If you suspect that this may occur, propose that the team develop more than one proposal.

- The team takes too long to finalize a decision, which can result in compromises and poor decisions being made. To avoid this situation, establish a time frame for when certain parts of the project must be completed. If meeting the deadline is just not possible, consider requesting additional time from upper management. However, be sure to provide upper management a specific time frame as to when the team believes the project will be completed.

- The team is over managed and not allowed to work as a team. If this should occur, contact the team leader or upper management about the situation and request to have the format of the team re-evaluated.

- Subgroups or alliances that have different goals or agendas are allowed to form within the team. If this should occur, try to bring the subgroup or alliance back in as part of the team. This can be accomplished by allowing the subgroup or alliance to present their proposal to the team for discussion. If that does not correct the problem, contact the team leader or upper management for assistance. In most cases, developing a new team may be the best alternative.

- The team is unable to visualize or accept change. When this occurs, the team leader or upper management may need to play a more active role in the team, such as providing the team a variety of proposals to evaluate and requesting an analysis of each option. If this does not resolve the situation, developing a new team may be the best alternative.

TELEPHONE COMMUNICATION

In the business world, telephones have replaced face-to-face conversations as the dominant form of verbal communication. Because of the important role that telephones serve in a business environment, it is essential that you understand how to use them effectively. This chapter will not only provide you the information you need to effectively communicate using a telephone, but also how to do so professionally.

1. TELEPHONE COMMUNICATION SKILLS

Unlike a face-to-face conversation where important information about a person can be gathered from body language and facial expressions, when communicating by telephone, the only method available to gather and provide information is from what is said and how it is said. Therefore, it is essential that you develop strong verbal communication skills when conversing by telephone. The tips provided below will assist you in the development of these skills.

- Speak in a clear and concise manner. Your goal when speaking is to ensure that the other person understands the information that you are providing.
- Avoid speaking too loudly or too softly. Instead, try to maintain a normal or cheerful tone when speaking.
- Maintain a positive and pleasant attitude even if you encounter an angry caller. Becoming angry will only escalate the caller's anger.

- Allow the other person to complete their sentence or thoughts prior to talking. Not only is this a common courtesy, but this also allows you to gather and evaluate all the information they are presenting to you which, in turn, will assist you in developing a proper response.

- Use confirming responses when the other person is speaking to reassure the caller that you are paying attention. Words such as, "yes," "sure," "ok," or "I understand" are great confirming responses.

- Assure the person you are talking to that you have their un-divided attention by not eating, drinking or completing other tasks while the conversation is taking place. In addition, minimize background noise. If you work in a busy office, you may find it helpful to close your door or inform others around you that you will be talking on the telephone prior to placing or answering a telephone call.

- Occasionally circumstances may exist that can cause you to have difficulty conversing, such as suffering from a cold. If so, consider completing the call at another time or completing the conversation through another form of communication, such as e-mail or fax.

- During the conversation, take notes on the information being discussed and any tasks that need to be completed.

- Before ending the call, summarize the conversation with the caller to ensure that you and the caller both agree on the information discussed and the tasks to be completed.

- When ending a call, always thank the other person for their time.

2. PLACING A CALL

Whether you are initiating a call or returning one, you need to be prepared for the call. In addition to using the tips provided in the previous section, the following tips will provide you suggestions on how to be prepared to place a call, as well as how to complete the call.

- Before placing a call, gather pertinent information you will need during the conversation. If you are returning a call, anticipate why the person called you and have the information available that you believe may be discussed. You may find it helpful to develop a list of topics you wish to be discussed to avoid the need for follow-up calls.

- Highlight the person's name that you are calling and place it in an obvious location on your notes so you can easily locate it should you forget the person's name during the conversation.

- Always be prepared to leave a message should the person you are calling not be available. You may find it helpful to refer to the "Leaving A Message Or Voicemail" section located in this chapter.
- When your call is answered, ensure that you are speaking to the correct person, identify yourself (your name, title, and organization you represent) and then state the reason for your telephone call. For example, "Hello, Mr. Smith, this is Bill Briefcase, Assistant Director of Marketing at XYZ, Inc. I am calling to discuss your recent advertising insertion."
- Before beginning the conversation, ask the other person if it is a convenient time for them to visit. If not, restate the purpose for your call, let them know how much time you anticipate the call taking, and request a time that would be more appropriate to call them. Always set a specific time for the return call to avoid delaying the conversation any further.
- Because you have initiated the call, it is your responsibility to begin the conversation. If appropriate, start the conversation with casual conversation to develop a rapport. However, if you sense that the person you are visiting with is busy, avoid engaging in casual conversation and proceed with the reason for your call. If you are returning a call, remind the person of their call and allow them to take over the responsibility of the call.
- Should you dial an incorrect number, do not hang up if someone answers. Instead, apologize for the mistake, inform them of the telephone number you had intended to call, and determine if you had misdialed the telephone number or if the telephone number you were provided is incorrect.

3. ANSWERING A CALL

As with placing a call, you need to be prepared when answering a call. This can be accomplished by implementing the tips provided in this section, as well those provided in the "Telephone Communication Skills" section located at the beginning of this chapter.

- Always have a note pad and pen available on your desk to take notes. Avoid using this note pad for other purposes so that you will not run out of paper or misplace it. In fact, you may find it helpful to keep a note pad under or next to your telephone for just this purpose.

- Before picking up the telephone, be sure you are ready to speak. If you need to clear your throat or have a drink of water, do so before lifting the phone off of the receiver so that the person calling does not hear you.
- Answer the telephone promptly, preferably before the third ring.
- Introduce yourself using your organization's preferred method of introduction. If your organization does not have a preferred method for answering calls, a standard introduction includes stating the name of the organization first and then your full name. For example, "XYZ, Inc. This is Bill Briefcase."
- As soon as the person provides you with their introduction, immediately write down their name, title and the organization they represent and the reason they are calling. If you did not get all of their information or you are unsure how to spell their name, ask them to repeat the information or spell their name before proceeding. Doing so will not only give the caller the perception that you value their call, but also helps you avoid addressing them incorrectly during the conversation.
- Should you need to leave the immediate area or need a few moments to review information in order to continue the conversation, ask the person if you can place them on hold. Be sure to let the person know how long you intend to put them on hold. When you return to the call, always thank them for holding. If gathering or reviewing the information is taking longer than you had anticipated, ask the person if you can call them back once you have a chance to gather or review all the information to avoid having them wait on the telephone any longer.
- Avoid disrupting the conversation by accepting other calls or talking to other people. However, if a situation arises where you must disrupt the call, offer an apology and briefly explain the reason for the disruption. If the disruption will be brief, ask if you can place them on hold for a moment. However, if the disruption will be for more than a minute, ask if you can return the call.
- Should you need to transfer a caller to another person, inform the caller that you will be transferring their call, who you will be transferring them to, as well as the telephone number for that person in case the caller wishes to contact that person at a later time.
- If your office has a receptionist, or if you have an assistant that screens your calls, take some time to inform that person how you would like your calls handled prior to the call being forwarded to you.

4. CONFERENCE CALLS & SPEAKERPHONE

Occasionally you may need to participate in a conference call or use the speakerphone option. Although conducting a conversation with these tools is very similar to conducting a conversation on a regular call, there are some important differences. The tips provided below will assist you in participating in a conference call or conducting a speakerphone conversation in a professional manner.

- Prior to participating in a conference call or conducting a speakerphone conversation, prepare the area where the call will be conducted to minimize background noises or interruptions.
- Before placing someone on speakerphone, always request the caller's permission. In addition, always inform the caller if other people will be participating or listening to the conversation.
- Each time you participate in a conference call conversation, identify yourself before proceeding. For example, "This is Robert again. I have also reviewed the 3rd quarter statements and..."
- Avoid creating disruptive noises, such as ruffling papers. Conference calls and speakerphone technologies have been developed to magnify sound in order for the other participants to hear you clearly. Therefore, any noises you make will be picked up and magnified to the other participants.
- Should an interruption occur during a conference call or during a speakerphone conversation, mute the call and handle the interruption as quickly as possible. If the interruption is obvious to the other participants, inform them of the interruption and let them know you will be placing your phone on mute while you resolve the interruption. When you do place your phone on mute, always be sure that your call is muted before proceeding with the interruption. This can be accomplished by asking the other participants if they can hear you. Doing so can help avoid a potentially embarrassing situation.

5. LEAVING A MESSAGE OR VOICEMAIL

Leaving a message or voicemail for someone is a fairly common task. However, far too often this task is conducted improperly. The following tips will ensure that messages and voicemails you leave are completed professionally and successfully.

- Speak slower than normal and focus on the clarity of your speech. This will ensure that the person collecting the information from the message understands what is being said.
- Always start and end the message or voicemail with your name and telephone number.
- Avoid leaving long detailed messages unless absolutely necessary. Simply provide the person your name and telephone number, the name of the organization you represent and the reason you are calling, and any other pertinent information.
- Never leave confidential information in a message or voicemail.
- If you require a response to your message or voicemail before a certain time, be sure to state that in the message or voicemail.

6. RECORDING A VOICEMAIL MESSAGE

Most businesses have voicemail features on their telephone systems. Should you be away from your office, even for a short amount of time, you need to provide callers the ability to leave you a message. Provided below are tips to assist you in recording a professional voicemail message.

- Before recording your voicemail, write down what you want the message to include so you do not leave out any information.
- Start your recording with your name, title, and the name of the organization you represent. This will inform the caller that they are leaving a voicemail for the correct person.
- Inform the caller when you will be listening to your voicemail. For example, if you are on vacation, inform the caller of this and when you will be returning to the office. However, if you just happen to be away from your desk for a short period of time, inform the caller that you are in the office and will be checking your voicemails when you return to your desk.
- Make your recording as brief as possible, but be sure to speak slowly and clearly when recording your voicemail to ensure that the caller hears all the information you are providing them.
- Ensure that your voicemail message is current to avoid confusing callers. You may find it helpful to record a new voicemail at the beginning of each workweek.
- If you will be away from the office for an extended period of time, offer the caller an option to speak with someone else in your office if they

need a more immediate response. For example, "If you would like to speak with someone else, please dial 0 and ask for ____."

- Listen to your voicemail after recording a new message to ensure it provides callers all the information that you had intended.

7. USING WIRELESS PHONES

Although the tips provided in this chapter also apply to using a wireless phone, there are a few specific points to keep in mind when using a wireless phone.

- Always evaluate your surroundings to ensure that the use of a wireless phone is appropriate. For example, are you in an area where the reception fades in and out, or speaking on your wireless phone may cause people around you to become annoyed?
- Use an appropriate ringer setting to inform you when a call is being received. For example, if you are in a quiet location, consider setting your wireless phone ringer to the vibration setting.
- Avoid using your wireless phone when driving as it can cause you to become distracted. If you must use your wireless phone when driving, invest in a hands-free system.
- Turn off your wireless phone when engaged in a conversation, meeting or other function where the use of a wireless phone would be distracting to you or to others. If you forget to turn off your phone and it rings, turn the phone off immediately and apologize for the distraction.

VACATION & SICK TIME

The policies and procedures related to a vacation and sick time program varies greatly from one organization to the next. For example, one organization may offer new employees a program that includes twelve vacation days and ten sick days per year, which starts being accrued immediately, yet the vacation time can only be used after the employee has completed their probationary period. Another organization may offer a combination vacation/sick program that includes twenty-two days per year that can be used as soon as it is accrued. This chapter will not only assist you in understanding your organization's vacation and sick time program, but also how to properly plan for, request, and return from your vacation and sick time.

1. REVIEW YOUR PROGRAM

As the examples above describe, a vacation and sick time program can vary greatly from one organization to the next. Therefore, it is in your best interest to contact your Human Resource Department, review your employee handbook, or contact your supervisor to get a clear understanding of your organization's vacation and sick time program. The following items highlight several important questions to answer as you review your organization's vacation and sick time program.

- How is your vacation and sick time accrued? For example, is it accumulated periodically throughout the year, such as per pay period, or is it provided in one lump sum at the beginning of the organization's fiscal year?

- Do blackout or probationary periods exist? For example, are there established times that vacation time cannot be used, such as during the peak sales season? Or is there a certain amount of time that you must work before you can use your accumulated vacation time, such as after a ninety day probationary period?

- What happens to unused vacation and sick time at the end of the year? For example, does the organization have a "use it or lose it policy," does it allow you to carry-over unused vacation and sick time into the next year, or does it pay employees for their unused vacation and sick time?

- Does the organization authorize vacation time based on seniority? For example, organizations with limited specialized staff, such as a hospital, may require that a certain number of staff be on hand to properly operate the facilities. Therefore, during popular holidays these organizations usually authorize vacation requests based on seniority.

- How are vacation and sick time requests authorized? For example, are you required to submit written requests for vacation time? If so, who authorizes the time and how soon does your request need to be submitted? If you need to use your sick time, what procedures must you follow?

- What is the policy for bereavement time? For example, some organizations grant their employees a specific amount of bereavement time, such as three days for the bereavement of an immediate family member. Under this situation, the bereavement time that is taken does not count against the employee's vacation or sick time. However, other organizations may count the time that is used for bereavement against the employee's vacation or sick time.

- What is the policy for paternity or maternity leave? Although state and federal laws usually mandate the amount of time used for paternity and maternity leave, the laws do vary depending on the size of the organization you work for. Therefore, you should consider consulting your state or federal representative for additional information.

- Can you take leave time without pay? In some situations, organizations may allow employees that have not accumulated a sufficient amount of vacation or sick time to take additional vacation or sick time without pay when special circumstances exist.

- Can pre-authorized vacation time be revoked? For example, if you requested and were granted vacation time and an emergency developed at the organization, some organizations have policies that give them the right to revoke pre-authorized vacation time. However, some organizations that have such policies in place also provide the employee compensation for expenses associated with revoking pre-authorized vacation time, such as expenses for airfare.

2. PLANNING FOR & REQUESTING VACATION TIME

To minimize disruption and potential conflicts, it is in your best interest to plan for and request your vacation time as soon as possible. The following bullet points offer several tips and suggestions to consider when planning for and requesting vacation time.

- If you plan to take an extended vacation within the first six months of being hired, inform the organization of your intentions before accepting the offer. Doing so will allow you to avoid potential conflicts after starting your new position.
- When requesting vacation time, always follow the organization's procedures for requesting the time to avoid potential conflicts, regardless of what someone else may have told you, including your supervisor.
- Choose extended vacation time during a period when your workload is reduced. Not only is your vacation time request more likely to be approved, but also you will have a minimal amount of pending work to deal with upon your return.
- When requesting vacation time near a major holiday, make your request as early as possible, as vacation time may be granted on a first-come first-serve basis.
- Always remember to respect your supervisor's authority, even when it comes to your vacation time. Although you have earned the vacation time, your supervisor still has the authority to authorize or decline your request. Therefore, never <u>tell</u> your supervisor that you are going to be using your vacation time; instead always request to use your vacation time.

3. PREPARING FOR & RETURNING FROM A VACATION

Using vacation time involves much more than just turning off the lights and leaving the office for a while. There are a number of issues that must be handled before you leave and after your return from a vacation. The following tips and suggestions will assist you in preparing for and returning from a vacation.

Preparing For A Vacation

- Remind your supervisor and coworkers of pre-authorized vacation time at least one week prior to leaving. This will allow them to prepare their schedules, as well as address any pending issues with you before you leave.
- Contact the person who will be filling in for you and update him on any pending issues that may need to be addressed while you are out.
- Change your voice mail and e-mail to inform people attempting to contact you that you are on vacation. Also be sure to include information about whom they can contact while you are out, as well as when you will be checking your messages.
- Finalize any pending projects to minimize your workload upon your return.
- Clean your desk and organize your office space prior to leaving for vacation to avoid documents and information from being misplaced while you are out.
- Make a list of pending issues to deal with upon your return to avoid forgetting something.
- If necessary, leave your contact information with your supervisor in case you need to be reached during your vacation.
- Be sure to leave your calendar clear of any appointments or meetings the day of your return to work to allow you the opportunity to catch up and take care of any pressing issues.

Returning From A Vacation

- Consider checking your voice mail and e-mail the night before returning to the office so you know what to be prepared for.
- Plan on staying after work for an hour or two a couple of days during the week that you return from vacation to allow you an opportunity to catch up.
- Remember to reset your e-mail and voice-mail accounts to inform people that you are back at work.

- Keep a log of the amount of vacation time you have used, and compare that with the amount of vacation time your supervisor or Human Resources Department reports you as using.

4. USING SICK TIME

Occasionally, there will be a time that you do not feel well enough to come into work. If so, be sure to consider the following tips and suggestions on how to properly use a sick day.

- Contact the person who has the authority to authorize your request for sick time as soon as possible. Be sure to contact that person in the manner authorized by the organization's policies and procedures, such as by telephone.
- Consider informing your supervisor where he can reach you in case he needs to contact you.
- Change your e-mail and voice mail features to inform people who are attempting to contact you that you are out of the office.
- Never lie to your supervisor about being sick in order to get a day off from work, as the risk of being caught and possibly losing your job is far too great.
- If you are sick, but have a project or assignment that needs to be completed as soon as possible, consider asking your boss if the information can be forwarded to you at home. This will allow you to work on it at home in the event that you feel better.

LIFE AFTER GRADUATION, LLC

Cofounders/Authors: Terry Arndt, MBA & John Ricchini, MBA, CPA
5645 Kathryn Street • Alexandria, VA 22303
(703) 960-4500 or (877) 569-9816
www.LifeAfterGraduation.com • info@LifeAfterGraduation.com

Our products provide students the tools they need to be successful during college, after graduation, and as they begin their new careers. Visit www.LifeAfterGraduation.com to learn more.

Life After Graduation provides a variety of financial advice and money saving tips, such as: understanding health insurance, purchasing a car, writing effective complaint letters, learning the basics of investing, developing an easy-to-follow budget, negotiating rent and requesting discounts from your landlord, moving on a budget, reducing your costs and maximizing your benefits when traveling.

Life During College provides a variety of valuable advice and tips for success, such as: selecting, scheduling and registering for courses, managing your time and money, taking effective lecturer notes, deciding where to live and signing a lease, selecting a major, studying for and taking exams, maintaining a healthy lifestyle, developing important campus safety skills, and preparing for your career.